全日本空手道剛柔会

剛柔流型教本

上巻

Japan Karatedo Gojukai Association
Goju-ryu Kata series (vol.1)

目次　Contents

はじめに

国際空手道剛柔会・全日本空手道剛柔会

会長 宗家　山口剛史

　本年２００９年は、全日本空手道剛柔会会祖山口剛玄先生が生誕されて１００周年記念の年であります。

　全日本空手道剛柔会及び山口宗家は、山口剛玄先生の生誕１００周年を記念して先生を偲び、生前のご功績を顕彰して記念行事を開催いたします。

　記念行事の一つとして、全日本空手道剛柔会宗家は剛柔流型全集をＤＶＤ及び教本として発行することになりました。

　近年、空手道は世界のスポーツとして広く普及されております。

　各国でオリンピック種目としての正式参加をスローガンに、明確な勝敗判定を規した競技化を進められておりますが、空手道がオリンピック種目として参加できる可能性は組手競技に限られると言われておりますのは誠に残念なことです。

　形は空手道そのものであり、空手道の流派、会派は全て形によって理念構成されていると言っても過言ではありません。

　オリンピックにおいて組手競技のみが採用された場合、これまで重用視された形の練習は疎かにされるでしょうし、組手競技参加のために型鍛錬の必要性がなくなったとしたら、それこそ空手道から武道性が欠如され、大きな損失となるでしょう。

　空手道は形の修練を通して自己鍛錬と天地人、天然の理を会得するのです。

　近代空手道が、流派を超越して空手道として統一されることは結構なことですが、当然、流派、会派による形の保存は重要な我々の義務と考えます。

　当教本は形を「型」として表現いたしますが、会祖山口剛玄先生が指導された全日本空手道剛柔会の制定型でまとめました。

　型の修練は正しい模範の模擬を通して上達いたします。

　イメージを高めて正しく修練されますことを心から切望いたします。

Introduction

International Karatedo Gojukai Association
Japan Karatedo Gojukai Association
President, Soke
Goshi Yamaguchi

The year 2009 marks the 100th anniversary of the birth of Gogen Yamaguchi Sensei, founder and grand master of the J.K.G.A.

The J.K.G.A. and the Yamaguchi family will be holding a memorial event this year to publicly honor and remember his services during his lifetime as well as commemorate the 100th anniversary of his birth.

As part of this event, the J.K.G.A. has published a complete guide to all of the Goju-ryu kata on DVD and in print.

In recent years, karate as a sport has become popular around the world.

Many countries are still pushing for karate to be recognized as an official Olympic event, it is unfortunate that only Kumite has the possibility of being recognized.

Kata is karate itself. It is no exaggeration to say that the philosophy of each style and organization is formed from their kata.

In the event that only Kumite is adopted into the Olympics, competitors will most likely neglect their kata training as they focus more on kumite traing, since kata will not be an Olympic event. I feel that this will be a great loss as it will remove many aspects of budo from karate.

In karate, we try to understand the relationship of between heaven, earth, and man through our practice of kata.

It is excellent that many styles and organizations will be unified by a modern karate, however I believe we have an important duty to preserve the kata of the individual styles and organizations.

In this manual kata is written with the character 型 and not 形 . Within it is a collection of J.K.G.A. kata which the founder and grand master Gogen Yamaguchi taught.

Kata training is improved through practice and imitation of an accurate model.

I wish from the bottom of my heart that you will improve your mental image of the kata and be able to practice them more accurately.

三戦

サンチン

Sanchin

型のポイント

　剛柔流を最も代表する基本型で、「転掌」と対をなし、呼吸法 " 息吹（いぶき）" を用いて基礎体力、筋力の強化、呼吸力、集中力を養い、剛柔流空手道修練に適した資質作りの型である。

　「三戦立ち」での前後、転身移動をもって、姿勢の維持、重心を落とした丹田集中による身体部位の締め、腹式呼吸による横隔膜の調整を図り、「天地人」の立禅境地を実践する。

　三戦立ちの前進移動は、内側向きの前足を踵から締め、前足を真っすぐにしてから後足を内側より床を擦るように前進させ、爪先を内側に向ける。

　" 息吹 " は陽・陰・半陽陰と異なる用法がある。用法は呼吸の強さ、身体の締めと弛緩の調整をもって使い分けることができる。

　「三戦」の型は通常は陽息吹の強い呼吸と諸筋肉の締めに合わせる。

　" 息吹 " の順序は、通常は呑（吸）と吐（呼）に分けるが、武術用法の呼吸として呑と吐の間に耐を入れ、吐の後に極で極める。

　突きの息吹は呑・耐・吐・極に合わせ、受けと構えは呑・吐・極に合わせる。

This is the most typical kata of Goju-ryu. Sanchin and Tensho are considered a pair. It is used for fundamental physical conditioning, building muscle strength, learning proper breathing, and concentration through a respiration method called IBUKI. Through this kata, one lays the foundation for learning the techniques of karate.

Keep correct posture while stepping and changing position in Sanchin, tense the body while focusing on Tanden and lowering center of gravity, and control the diaphragm with abdominal respiration. Practicing Sanchin is the same as practicing standing Zen while contemplating the meaning of " heaven, earth, and man."

When stepping forward in Sanchin Dachi, first point the front foot forward by moving the heel inside. Second, slide the back foot forward along the floor, pointing the toes inside.

There are 3 different methods of Ibuki: Yo, In, Han-yo-in. Each method differs in the force of breathing as well as the tension and relaxation of the body. Normally, Sanchin kata is performed with Yo Ibuki, (strong breathing) and tension of the muscle. Ibuki is divided into Don(inhale) and To(exhale). In the method of breathing for martial arts, Tai(pause) comes between Don and To, and Kyoku(kime or focus) comes after To.

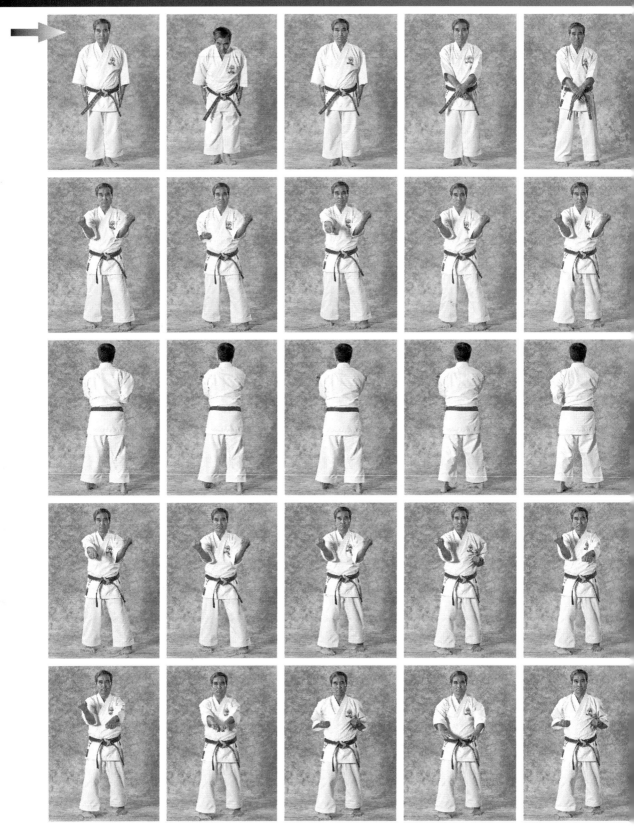

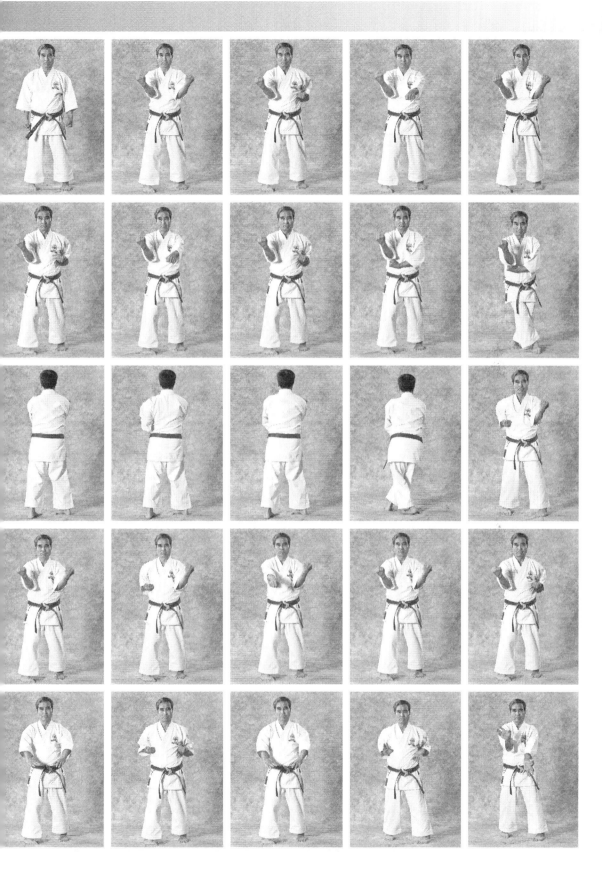

気を付け　　　　　礼　　　　　結び立ち

立ち方●結び立ち
注意点●顎を引き、両手は真っすぐ
伸ばして大腿側部につける
Stance ● Musubidachi
Point ● Pull chin back. Keep
fingers straight and hands on
outer thight.

立ち方●結び立ち
注意点●前方30度位、礼は深すぎ
ない
Stance ● Musubidachi
Point ● Bow forward for 30°.Be
careful not to bow too deeply

立ち方●結び立ち
Stance ● Musubidachi

裏側

【小手合わせ】　　Kote Awase

用意1	用意2	用意3

中間動作

裏側

立ち方●結び立ち
注意点●右掌内側、丹田の前で重ね集中
息吹●ゆっくり呑
Stance ● Musubidachi
Point ● Right hand on the inside. Hands are crossed in front of Tanden
Ibuki ● Inhale slowly

立ち方●平行立ち
注意点●爪先を支点に踵を外に開く
Stance ● Heiko Dachi
Point ● Keep balls of feet in place and only move heels.

立ち方●平行立ち
注意点●両拳は脇を締めながら体側へ、正拳は真下へ向けて、両肩を落とす
息吹●ゆっくり吐
Stance ● Heiko Dachi
Point ● Keep elbows against side of body, fists pointing straight down, and shoulders relaxed
Ibuki ● Exhale slowly

第１挙動	第２挙動	第３挙動

裏側

立ち方●右三戦立ち
技●右腕を外側より両手中段受け・三戦構え
注意点●右足を内側より一歩前進
Stance ● Right Sanchin Dachi
Tech. ● Double arm Chudan Uke into Sanchin kamae. When blocking, right arm is on the outside

立ち方●右三戦立ち
技●左拳引き手
息吹●呑
Stance ● Right Sanchin Dachi
Tech. ● Left Hikite
Ibuki ● Inhale

立ち方●右三戦立ち
技●左拳正拳突き
注意点●突きは左中心線
息吹●吐
Stance ● Right Sanchin Dachi
Tech. ● Left Seiken Tsuki
Point ● Punch is in center of left half of body
Ibuki ● Exhale

第4挙動	第5挙動	第6挙動

中間動作

裏側

立ち方●右三戦立ち
技●左腕中段受け
注意点●左腕にて左中心線を受ける
息吹●呑吐
Stance ● Right Sanchin Dachi
Tech. ● Left Chudan Uke
Ibuki ● Inhale and exhale

立ち方●左足を内側より一歩前進
Stance ● Step forward w/ left foot using an inward curve

立ち方●左三戦立ち
技●右拳引き手
息吹●呑
Stance ● Left Sanchin Dachi
Tech. ● Right Hikite
Ibuki ● Inhale

第７挙動　　　　第８挙動　　　　第９挙動

立ち方●左三戦立ち
技●右拳正拳突き
注意点●突きは右中心線
息吹●吐
Stance ● Left Sanchin Dachi
Tech. ● Right Seiken Tsuki
Point ● Punch is in center of right half of body
Ibuki ● Exhale

立ち方●左三戦立ち
技●右中段受け
注意点●右腕にて右中心線を受ける
息吹●呑吐
Stance ● Left Sanchin Dachi
Tech. ● Right Chudan Uke
Point ● Block is in center of right half of body
Ibuki ● Inhale and exhale

立ち方●右足を内側より一歩前進
Stance ● Step forward w/ right foot using an inward curve

第 10 挙動	第 11 挙動	第 12 挙動

中間動作

裏側

立ち方●右三戦立ち	立ち方●右三戦立ち	立ち方●右三戦立ち
技●左拳引き手	技●左拳正拳突き	技●左拳引き手
息吹●呑	息吹●吐	息吹●呑
Stance ● Right Sanchin Dachi	Stance ● Right Sanchin Dachi	Stance ● Right Sanchin Dachi
Tech. ● Left Hikite	Tech. ● Left Seiken Tsuki	Tech. ● Left Hikite
Ibuki ● Inhale	Ibuki ● Exhale	Ibuki ● Inhale

第 13 挙動　　　　第 14 挙動　　　　第 15 挙動

裏側

立ち方●右三戦立ち
技●左拳で右肘下まで突き
息吹●吐
Stance ● Right Sanchin Dachi
Tech. ● Punch w/ left fist under
right elbow
Ibuki ● Exhale

立ち方●右足を左側へ移動
Stance ● Cross legs (Put right
foot over the left)

立ち方●方向を転回、左三戦立ち
技●左腕にて中段受け
息吹●呑
Stance ● Turn around into left
Sanchin Dachi
Tech. ● Left Chudan Uke
Ibuki ● Inhale

第 16 挙動	第 17 挙動	第 18 挙動

中間動作

裏側

立ち方●左三戦立ち
技●右拳正拳突き
息吹●吐
Stance ● Left Sanchin Dachi
Tech. ● Right Seiken Tsuki
Ibuki ● Exhale

立ち方●左三戦立ち
技●右腕で中段受け
息吹●呑吐
Stance ● Left Sanchin Dachi
Tech. ● Chudan Uke w/ right arm
Ibuki ● Inhale and exhale

立ち方●右足を一歩前進、三戦立ち
Stance ● Step forward w/ right foot into Sanchin Dachi

第 19 挙動　　　第 20 挙動　　　第 21 挙動

裏側

立ち方●右三戦立ち
技●左拳引き手
息吹●呑
Stance ● Right Sanchin Dachi
Tech. ● Left Hikite
Ibuki ● Inhale

立ち方●右三戦立ち
技●左拳正拳突き
息吹●吐
Stance ● Right Sanchin Dachi
Tech. ● Left Seiken Tsuki
Ibuki ● Exhale

立ち方●右三戦立ち
技●左拳引き手
息吹●呑
Stance ● Right Sanchin Dachi
Tech. ● Left Hikite
Ibuki ● Inhale

第 22 挙動	第 23 挙動	第 24 挙動

中間動作

裏側

立ち方●右三戦立ち
技●左拳で右肘下まで突き
息吹●吐
Stance ● Right Sanchin Dachi
Tech. ● Punch w/ left fist under right elbow
Ibuki ● Exhale

立ち方●右足を左側へ移動
Stance ● Cross legs (Put right foot over the left)

立ち方●方向を転回、左三戦立ち
技●左腕にて中段受け
息吹●呑
Stance ● Turn around into left Sanchin Dachi
Tech. ● Left Chudan Uke
Ibuki ● Inhale

第 25 挙動	第 26 挙動	第 27 挙動

裏側

立ち方●左三戦立ち
技●右拳正拳突き
息吹●吐
Stance ● Left Sanchin Dachi
Tech. ● Right Seiken Tsuki
Ibuki ● Exhale

立ち方●左三戦立ち
技●右腕中段受け
息吹●呑吐
Stance ● Left Sanchin Dachi
Tech. ● Right Chudan Uke
Ibuki ● Inhale and exhale

立ち方●右足を一歩前進、三戦立ち
Stance ● Step forward w/ right
foot into Sanchin Dachi

第 28 挙動	第 29 挙動	第 30 挙動

中間動作

裏側

立ち方●右三戦立ち	立ち方●右三戦立ち	立ち方●右三戦立ち
技●左拳引き手	技●左拳正拳突き	技●左腕中段受け
息吹●呑	息吹●吐	息吹●呑吐
Stance ● Right Sanchin Dachi	Stance ● Right Sanchin Dachi	Stance ● Right Sanchin Dachi
Tech. ● Left Hikite	Tech. ● Left Seiken Tsuki	Tech. ● Left Chudan Uke
Ibuki ● Inhale	Ibuki ● Exhale	Ibuki ● Inhale and exhale

裏側

立ち方●右三戦立ち	立ち方●右三戦立ち	立ち方●右三戦立ち
技●右拳引き手	技●右拳正拳突き	技●右腕中段受け
息吹●呑	息吹●吐	息吹●呑吐
Stance ● Right Sanchin Dachi	Stance ● Right Sanchin Dachi	Stance ● Right Sanchin Dachi
Tech. ● Right Hikite	Tech. ● Right Seiken Tsuki	Tech. ● Right Chudan Uke
Ibuki ● Inhale	Ibuki ● Exhale	Ibuki ● Inhale and exhale

第34挙動	第35挙動	第36挙動

中間動作

裏側

立ち方●右三戦立ち
技●左拳引き手
息吹●呑
Stance ● Right Sanchin Dachi
Tech. ● Left Hikite
Ibuki ● Inhale

立ち方●右三戦立ち
技●左拳正拳突き
息吹●吐
Stance ● Right Sanchin Dachi
Tech. ● Left Seiken Tsuki
Ibuki ● Exhale

立ち方●右三戦立ち
技●両手開手
Stance ● Right Sanchin Dachi
Tech. ● Open both hands

第37挙動　　　　　第38挙動　　　　　第39挙動

裏側

立ち方●右三戦立ち
技●両手引き手
息吹●呑
Stance ● Right Sanchin Dachi
Tech. ● Hikite w/ both arms
Ibuki ● Inhale

立ち方●右三戦立ち
技●両手開手張り突き
息吹●吐
Stance ● Right Sanchin Dachi
Tech. ● Harizuki w/ both hands open
Ibuki ● Exhale

立ち方●右三戦立ち
技●両手引き手
息吹●呑
Stance ● Right Sanchin Dachi
Tech. ● Hikite w/ both arms
Ibuki ● Inhale

第 40 挙動	第 41 挙動	第 42 挙動

中間動作

裏側

立ち方●右三戦立ち	立ち方●右三戦立ち	立ち方●右三戦立ち
技●両手開手張り突き	技●両手引き手	技●両手開手張り突き
息吹●吐	息吹●呑	息吹●吐
Stance ● Right Sanchin Dachi	Stance ● Right Sanchin Dachi	Stance ● Right Sanchin Dachi
Tech. ● Open hands Harizuki	Tech. ● Hikite w/ both arms	Tech. ● Open hands Harizuki
Ibuki ● Exhale	Ibuki ● Inhale	Ibuki ● Exhale

第43挙動	第44挙動	第45挙動

裏側

立ち方●右足一歩後退、左三戦立ち	立ち方●左三戦立ち	立ち方●左足一歩後退、右三戦立ち
技●右から廻し受け	技●両手底掌当て	技●左から廻し受け
息吹●呑	息吹●吐	息吹●呑
Stance ● Step back w/ right foot into left Sanchin Dachi	Stance ● Left Sanchin Dachi	Stance ● Step back w/ left foot into right Sanchin Dachi
Tech. ● Mawashiuke w/ right hand on top	Tech. ● Teisho Ate w/ right hand on top	Tech. ● Mawashiuke w/ left hand top
Ibuki ● Inhale	Ibuki ● Exhale	Ibuki ● Inhale

第46挙動	直って	直って

中間動作

裏側

| 立ち方●右三戦立ち
技●両手底掌当て
息吹●吐
Stance ● Right Sanchin Dachi
Tech. ● Teisho Ate w/ left hand on top
Ibuki ● Exhale | 立ち方●前足を引いて結び立ち
技●右手掌上に重ねる
息吹●呑
Stance ● Step back w/ right foot into Musubidachi
Tech. ● Place right hand on top of left
Ibuki ● Inhale | 立ち方●結び立ち
技●手掌を摺り合わせて丹田集中
息吹●吐
Stance ● Musubidachi
Tech. ● Bring hands down in front of Tanden
Ibuki ● Exhale |

気を付け	礼	気を付け

裏側

立ち方●結び立ち
注意点●顎を引き、両手は真っすぐ伸ばして大腿側部に付ける
Stance ● Musubidachi
Point ● Pull chin back. Keep fingers straight and hands on outer thight.

立ち方●結び立ち
注意点●前方30度位、礼は深すぎない
Stance ● Musubidachi
Point ● Bow forward for 30° .Be careful not to bow too deeply

立ち方●結び立ち
注意点●顎を引き、両手は真っすぐ伸ばして大腿側部に付ける
Stance ● Musubidachi
Point ● Pull chin back. Keep fingers straight and hands on outer thight.

太極
上段2

タイキョク
ジョウダン2
Taikyoku Jodan 2

型のポイント

　「太極上段」から「太極廻し受け」までの「太極」の型は、会祖 山口剛玄先生によって制定された型で、「ゲキサイ第1・第2」に進む初心者用の練習型である。「ゲキサイ」の型を含めて「普及型」と呼ぶ。

　「太極上段」は「太極上段1」と「太極上段2」に分ける。

　「太極上段1」は「受け」「突き」を共に三戦立ちで行い、「太極上段2」は「受け」を三戦立ち、「突き」を前屈立ちで行う。「太極上段1及び2」の「受け」は上段受け（別名上受け）、「突き」は上段正拳突きで、「受け」「突き」の移動転身は素早く行う。

　【太極】とは移動転身をする演武線を言い、スタート位置での"用意"から"直れ"まで1〜19の挙動動作を演武する。

The Taikyoku kata from Taikyoku Jodan to Taikyoku Mawashiuke were created by Gogen Yamaguchi Sensei, the founder of J.K.G.A.

Beginners first practice Taikyoku kata before learning Gekisai Dai-ichi and Gekisai Dai-ni. The Taikyoku and Gekisai kata are called "Fukyu kata" (kata for propagation).

Taikyoku Jodan is divided into two versions.　In Taikyoku Jodan 1, both blocks and punches are performed in Sanchin Dachi. In Taikyoku Jodan 2, blocks are performed in Sanchin Dachi while punches are performed in Zenkutsu dachi.

All blocks are Jodan Uke and all punches are Jodan Seiken Tsuki.

All steps in the kata are performed quickly.

The word "Taikyoku" means the directions of movement. There are 19 movements in Taikyoku Jodan, from "Heiko Dachi Yōi" at the starting position to "Naore."

気を付け　　　　　礼　　　　　気を付け

中間動作

裏側

立ち方●結び立ち
注意点●顎を引き、両手は真っすぐ
伸ばして大腿側部につける
Stance ● Musubidachi
Point ● Pull chin back. Keep
fingers straight and hands on
outer thight.

立ち方●結び立ち
注意点●前方30度位、礼は深すぎ
ない
Stance ● Musubidachi
Point ● Bow forward for 30°.Be
careful not to bow too deeply

立ち方●結び立ち
Stance ● Musubidachi

用意1 　　　用意2 　　　用意3

立ち方●結び立ち
注意点●右掌内側、丹田の前で重ね
丹田集中
息吹●ゆっくり呑
Stance ● Musubidachi
Point ● Right hand on the
inside. Hands are crossed in
front of Tanden
Ibuki ● Inhale slowly

立ち方●平行立ち
注意点●爪先を支点に踵を外に開く
Stance ● Heiko Dachi
Point ● Keep balls of feet in
place and only move heels

立ち方●平行立ち
注意点●両拳は脇を締めながら体側
へ、正拳は真下へ向けて、両肩を落
とす
息吹●ゆっくり吐
Stance ● Heiko Dachi
Point ● Keep elbows against
side of body, fists pointing
straight down, and shoulders
relaxed
Ibuki ● Exhale slowly

第1挙動	第2挙動	第3挙動

中間動作

裏側

| 立ち方●左三戦立ち
技●左上段受け
Stance ● Left Sanchin Dachi
Tech. ● Left Jodan Uke | 立ち方●右前屈立ち
技●右上段正拳突き
Stance ● Right Zenkutsu Dachi
Tech. ● Right Jodan Tsuki | 立ち方●右三戦立ち
技●右上段受け
Stance ● Right Sanchin Dachi
Tech. ● Right Jodan Uke |

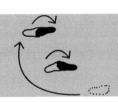

第４挙動	第５挙動	第６挙動

裏側

立ち方●左前屈立ち	立ち方●左三戦立ち	立ち方●右前屈立ち
技●左上段正拳突き	技●左上段受け	技●右上段正拳突き
Stance ● Left Zenkutsu Dachi	Stance ● Left Sanchin Dachi	Stance ● Right Zenkutsu Dachi
Tech. ● Left Jodan Tsuki	Tech. ● Left Jodan Uke	Tech. ● Right Jodan Tsuki

第7挙動	第8挙動	第9挙動

中間動作

裏側

立ち方●左前屈立ち
技●左上段正拳突き
Stance ● Left Zenkutsu Dachi
Tech. ● Left Jodan Tsuki

立ち方●右前屈立ち
技●右上段正拳突き
注意点●気合
Stance ● Right Zenkutsu Dachi
Tech. ● Right Jodan Tsuki
Point ● Kiai

立ち方●左三戦立ち
技●左上段受け
Stance ● Left Sanchin Dachi
Tech. ● Left Jodan Uke

第 10 挙動	第 11 挙動	第 12 挙動

裏側

立ち方●右前屈立ち
技●右上段正拳突き
Stance ● Right Zenkutsu Dachi
Tech. ● Right Jodan Tsuki

立ち方●右三戦立ち
技●右上段受け
Stance ● Right Sanchin Dachi
Tech. ● Right Jodan Uke

立ち方●左前屈立ち
技●左上段正拳突き
Stance ● Left Zenkutsu Dachi
Tech. ● Left Jodan Tsuki

第 13 挙動	第 14 挙動	第 15 挙動

中間動作

裏側

立ち方●左三戦立ち
技●左上段受け
Stance ● Left Sanchin Dachi
Tech. ● Left Jodan Uke

立ち方●右前屈立ち
技●右上段正拳突き
Stance ● Right Zenkutsu Dachi
Tech. ● Right Jodan Tsuki

立ち方●左前屈立ち
技●左上段正拳突き
Stance ● Left Zenkutsu Dachi
Tech. ● Left Jodan Tsuki

第16挙動	第17挙動	第18挙動

 裏側

立ち方●右前屈立ち
技●右上段正拳突き
注意点●気合
Stace ● Right Zenkutsu Dachi
Tech. ● Right Jodan Tsuki
Point ● Kiai

立ち方●左三戦立ち
技●左上段受け
Stance ● Left Sanchin Dachi
Tech. ● Left Jodan Uke

立ち方●右前屈立ち
技●右上段正拳突き
Stace ● Right Zenkutsu Dachi
Tech. ● Right Jodan Tsuki

第19挙動	直って	直って

裏側

立ち方●右三戦立ち
技●右上段受け
注意点●受けはゆっくり
Stace ● Right Sanchin Dachi
Tech. ● Right Jodan Uke
Point ● Block slowly

立ち方●前足を引いて結び立ち
技●右手掌上に重ねる
息吹●呑
Stance ● Step back w/ right foot into Musubidachi
Tech. ● Place right hand on top of left
Ibuki ● Inhale

立ち方●結び立ち
技●手掌を摺り合わせて丹田集中
息吹●吐
Stance ● Musubidachi
Tech. ● Bring hands down in front of Tanden
Ibuki ● Exhale

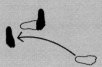

気を付け	礼	気を付け

裏側

立ち方●結び立ち
注意点●顎を引き、両手は真っすぐ
伸ばして大腿側部に付ける
Stance ● Musubidachi
Point ● Pull chin back. Keep
fingers straight and hands on
outer thight.

立ち方●結び立ち
注意点●前方30度位、礼は深すぎ
ない
Stance ● Musubidachi

立ち方●結び立ち
注意点●顎を引き、両手は真っすぐ
伸ばして大腿側部に付ける
Stance ● Musubidachi
Point ● Pull chin back. Keep
fingers straight and hands on
outer thight.

太極中段 2

タイキョク
チュウダン 2
Taikyoku
Chudan 2

型のポイント

「太極上段1及び2」と同じく初心者の型として制定され、1と2に分ける。

「太極中段1」は「受け」「突き」を共に前屈立ちで移動転身し、「太極中段2」は「受け」を三戦立ち、「突き」を前屈立ちで移動転身させる。

「太極中段1及び2」の「受け」は中段受け（別名 横受け）、「突き」は中段正拳突きで移動は素早く行う。

「太極」とは、移動転身する演武線を言い、スタート位置 "用意" から "直れ" まで1～19の挙動動作を演武する。

Taikyoku Chudan was also created as a kata for beginners and is divided into two different versions, "Taikyoku Chudan 1" and "2."

Taikyoku Chudan 1, both blocks and punches are performed in Zenkutsu dachi. In Taikyoku Chudan 2, blocks are performed in Sanchin Dachi while punches are performed in Zenkutsu dachi.

All blocks are Chudan Uke (can also be called Yoko Uke) and all punches are Chudan Seiken Tsuki. All steps in the kata are performed quickly.

The word "Taikyoku" means the direction of movement. There are 19 movements in Taikyoku Chudan, from "Heiko Dachi Yōi" at the starting position to "Naore."

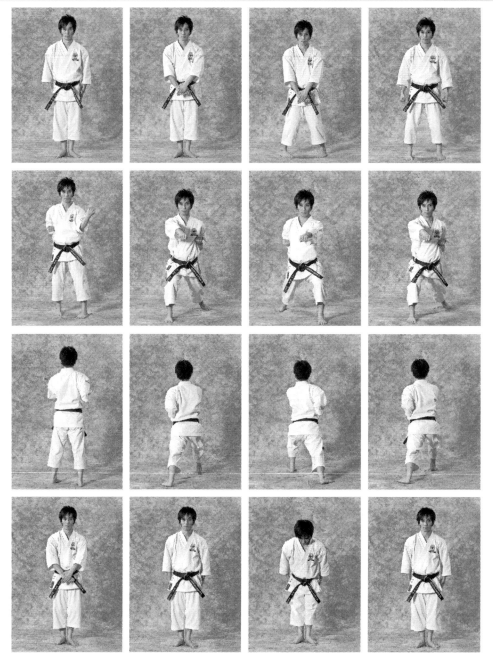

気を付け	礼	気を付け

中間動作

裏側

立ち方●結び立ち
注意点●顎を引き、両手は真っすぐ
伸ばして大腿側部につける
Stance ● Musubidachi
Point ● Pull chin back. Keep
fingers straight and hands on
outer thight.

立ち方●結び立ち
注意点●前方30度位、礼は深すぎ
ない
Stance ● Musubidachi
Point ● Bow forward for 30°.Be
careful not to bow too deeply

立ち方●結び立ち
Stance ● Musubidachi

用意1　　　用意2　　　用意3

裏側

立ち方●結び立ち
注意点●右掌内側、丹田の前で重ね
丹田集中
息吹●ゆっくり呑
Stance ● Musubidachi
Point ● Right hand on the inside. Hands are crossed in front of Tanden
Ibuki ● Inhale slowly

立ち方●平行立ち
注意点●爪先を支点に踵を外に開く
Stance ● Heiko Dachi
Point ● Keep balls of feet in place and only move heels

立ち方●平行立ち
注意点●両拳は脇を締めながら体側へ、正拳は真下へ向けて、両肩を落とす
息吹●ゆっくり吐
Stance ● Heiko Dachi
Point ● Keep elbows against side of body, fists pointing straight down, and shoulders relaxed
Ibuki ● Exhale slowly

第１挙動	第２挙動	第３挙動

中間動作

裏側

立ち方●左三戦立ち 技●左中段受け Stance ● Left Sanchin Dachi Tech. ● Left Chudan Uke	立ち方●右前屈立ち 技●右中段正拳突き Stance ● Right Zenkutsu Dachi Tech. ● Right Chudan Tsuki	立ち方●右三戦立ち 技●右中段受け Stance ● Right Sanchin Dachi Tech. ● Right Chudan Uke

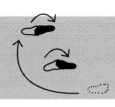

第４挙動	第５挙動	第６挙動

立ち方●左前屈立ち	立ち方●左三戦立ち	立ち方●右前屈立ち
技●左中段正拳突き	技●左中段受け	技●右中段正拳突き
Stance ● Left Zenkutsu Dachi	Stance ● Left Sanchin Dachi	Stance ● Right Zenkutsu Dachi
Tech. ● Left Chudan Tsuki	Tech. ● Left Chudan Uke	Tech. ● Right Chudan Tsuki

第7挙動	第8挙動	第9挙動

中間動作

裏側

立ち方●左前屈立ち
技●左中段正拳突き
Stance ● Left Zenkutsu Dachi
Tech. ● Left Chudan Tsuki

立ち方●右前屈立ち
技●右中段正拳突き
注意点●気合
Stance ● Right Zenkutsu Dachi
Tech. ● Right Chudan Tsuki
Point ● Kiai

立ち方●左三戦立ち
技●左中段受け
Stance ● Left Sanchin Dachi
Tech. ● Left Chudan Uke

第10挙動	第11挙動	第12挙動

裏側

立ち方●右前屈立ち	立ち方●右三戦立ち	立ち方●左前屈立ち
技●右中段正拳突き	技●右中段受け	技●左中段正拳突き
Stance ● Right Zenkutsu Dachi	Stance ● Right Sanchin Dachi	Stance ● Left Zenkutsu Dachi
Tech. ● Right Chudan Tsuki	Tech. ● Right Chudan Uke	Tech. ● Left Chudan Tsuki

 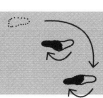 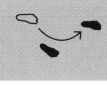

第 13 挙動	第 14 挙動	第 15 挙動

中間動作

裏側

立ち方●左三戦立ち
技●左中段受け

Stance ● Left Sanchin Dachi
Tech. ● Left Chudan Uke

立ち方●右前屈立ち
技●右中段正拳突き

Stance ● Right Zenkutsu Dachi
Tech. ● Right Chudan Tsuki

立ち方●左前屈立ち
技●左中段正拳突き

Stance ● Left Zenkutsu Dachi
Tech. ● Left Chudan Tsuki

第 16 挙動　　　　第 17 挙動　　　　第 18 挙動

裏側

立ち方●右前屈立ち
技●右中段正拳突き
注意点●気合
Stance ● Right Zenkutsu Dachi
Tech. ● Right Chudan Tsuki
Point ● Kiai

立ち方●左三戦立ち
技●左中段受け
Stance ● Left Sanchin Dachi
Tech. ● Left Chudan Uke

立ち方●右前屈立ち
技●右中段正拳突き
Stance ● Right Zenkutsu Dachi
Tech. ● Right Chudan Tsuki

第 19 挙動	直って	直って

裏側

立ち方●右三戦立ち
技●右中段受け
注意点●受けはゆっくり
Stance ● Right Sanchin Dachi
Tech. ● Right Chudan Uke
Point ● Block slowly

立ち方●前足を引いて結び立ち
技●右手掌上に重ねる
息吹●呑
Stance ● Step back w/ right
foot into Musubidachi
Tech. ● Place right hand on top
of left
Ibuki ● Inhale

立ち方●結び立ち
技●手掌を摺り合わせて丹田集中
息吹●吐
Stance ● Musubidachi
Tech. ● Bring hands down in
front of Tanden
Ibuki ● Exhale

気を付け　　礼　　気を付け

裏側

立ち方●結び立ち
注意点●顎を引き、両手は真っすぐ
伸ばして大腿側部に付ける
Stance ● Musubidachi
Point ● Pull chin back. Keep
fingers straight and hands on
outer thight.

立ち方●結び立ち
注意点●前方30度位、礼は深すぎ
ない
Stance ● Musubidachi
Point ● Bow forward for 30° .Be
careful not to bow too deeply

立ち方●結び立ち
注意点●顎を引き、両手は真っすぐ
伸ばして大腿側部に付ける
Stance ● Musubidachi
Point ● Pull chin back. Keep
fingers straight and hands on
outer thight.

太極下段 1

タイキョクゲダン 1

Taikyoku
Gedan 1

型のポイント

　「太極下段１」は「受け」「突き」共に四股立ち斜角（45度）で移動転身し、「太極下段２」は「受け」を四股立ち斜角で転身し、「突き」を四股立ち直角（90度）で移動させる。

　「太極下段１及び２」の「受け」は下段払い（別名 払い落とし）、「突き」は中段正拳突きで、移動転身は素早く行う。

　「太極」とは移動転身する演武線を言い、スタート位置 "用意" から " 直れ " まで１〜19の挙動動作を演武する。

In Taikyoku Gedan 1, blocks and punches are performed in Shiko Dachi 45°.
In Taikyoku Gedan 2, blocks are performed in Shiko Dachi 45° while punches are performed in Shiko Dachi 90°.
All blocks are Gedan Barai (can also be called Harai Otoshi) and all punches are Chudan Seiken Tsuki. All steps in the kata are performed quickly.
The word "Taikyoku" means the direction of movement. There are 19 movements in Taikyoku Gedan, from "Heiko Dachi Yōi" at the starting position to "Naore."

気を付け	礼	気を付け

中間動作

裏側

立ち方●結び立ち
注意点●顎を引き、両手は真っすぐ
伸ばして大腿側部につける
Stance ● Musubidachi
Point ● Pull chin back. Keep
fingers straight and hands on
outer thight.

立ち方●結び立ち
注意点●前方30度位、礼は深すぎ
ない
Stance ● Musubidachi
Point ● Bow forward for 30° .Be
careful not to bow too deeply

立ち方●結び立ち
Stance ● Musubidachi

用意１　用意２　用意３

立ち方●結び立ち
注意点●右掌内側、丹田の前で重ね
丹田集中
息吹●ゆっくり呑
Stance ● Musubidachi
Point ● Right hand on the inside. Hands are crossed in front of Tanden
Ibuki ● Inhale slowly

立ち方●平行立ち
注意点●爪先を支点に踵を外に開く
Stance ● Heiko Dachi
Point ● Keep balls of feet in place and only move heels

立ち方●平行立ち
注意点●両拳は脇を締めながら体側へ、正拳は真下へ向けて、両肩を落とす
息吹●ゆっくり吐
Stance ● Heiko Dachi
Point ● Keep elbows against side of body, fists pointing straight down, and shoulders relaxed
Ibuki ● Exhale slowly

裏側

第１挙動	第２挙動	第３挙動

中間動作

裏側

立ち方●左四股立ち斜角
技●左下段払い
Stance ● Left Shiko Dachi 45°
Tech. ● Left Gedan Barai

立ち方●右四股立ち斜角
技●右中段正拳突き
Stance ● Right Shiko Dachi 45°
Tech. ● Right Chudan Tsuki

立ち方●右四股立ち斜角
技●右下段払い
Stance ● Right Shiko Dachi 45°
Tech. ● Right Gedan Barai

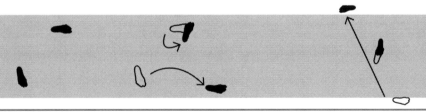

第4挙動　　　第5挙動　　　第6挙動

裏側

立ち方●左四股立ち斜角
技●左中段正拳突き
Stance ● Left Shiko Dachi 45°
Tech. ● Left Chudan Tsuki

立ち方●左四股立ち斜角
技●左下段払い
Stance ● Left Shiko Dachi 45°
Tech. ● Left Gedan Barai

立ち方●右四股立ち斜角
技●右中段正拳突き
Stance ● Right Shiko Dachi 45°
Tech. ● Right Chudan Tsuki

 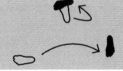

第7挙動	第8挙動	第9挙動

 中間動作

 裏側

立ち方●左四股立ち斜角
技●左中段正拳突き
Stance ● Left Shiko Dachi 45°
Tech. ● Left Chudan Tsuki

立ち方●右四股立ち斜角
技●右中段正拳突き
注意点●気合
Stance ● Right Shiko Dachi 45°
Tech. ● Right Chudan Tsuki
Point ● Kiai

立ち方●左四股立ち斜角
技●左下段払い
Stance ● Left Shiko Dachi 45°
Tech. ● Left Gedan Barai

  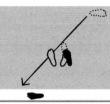

第10挙動　　　　　第11挙動　　　　　第12挙動

立ち方●右四股立ち斜角
技●右中段正拳突き
Stance ● Right Shiko Dachi 45°
Tech. ● Right Chudan Tsuki

立ち方●右四股立ち斜角
技●右下段払い
Stance ● Right Shiko Dachi 45°
Tech. ● Right Gedan Barai

立ち方●左四股立ち斜角
技●左中段正拳突き
Stance ● Left Shiko Dachi 45°
Tech. ● Left Chudan Tsuki

裏側

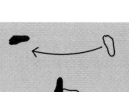 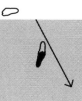 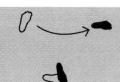

第 13 挙動	第 14 挙動	第 15 挙動

中間動作

裏側

立ち方●左四股立ち斜角
技●左下段払い
Stance ● Left Shiko Dachi 45°
Tech. ● Left Gedan Barai

立ち方●右四股立ち斜角
技●右中段正拳突き
Stance ● Right Shiko Dachi 45°
Tech. ● Right Chudan Tsuki

立ち方●左四股立ち斜角
技●左中段正拳突き
Stance ● Left Shiko Dachi 45°
Tech. ● Left Chudan Tsuki

第 16 挙動	第 17 挙動	第 18 挙動

			裏側

立ち方●右四股立ち斜角
技●右中段正拳突き
注意点●気合
Stance ● Right Shiko Dachi 45°
Tech. ● Right Chudan Tsuki
Point ● Kiai

立ち方●左四股立ち斜角
技●左下段払い
Stance ● Left Shiko Dachi 45°
Tech. ● Left Gedan Barai

立ち方●右四股立ち斜角
技●右中段正拳突き
Stance ● Right Shiko Dachi 45°
Tech. ● Right Chudan Tsuki

 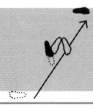 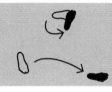

第19挙動	直って	直って

中間動作

裏側

立ち方●右四股立ち斜角
技●右下段払い
注意点●下段払いはゆっくり
Stance ● Right Shiko Dachi 45°
Tech. ● Right Gedan Barai
Point ● Block slowly

立ち方●前足を引いて結び立ち
技●右手掌上に重ねる
息吹●呑
Stance ● Step back w/ right foot into Musubidachi
Tech. ● Place right hand on top of left
Ibuki ● Inhale

立ち方●結び立ち
技●手掌を摺り合わせて丹田集中
息吹●吐
Stance ● Musubidachi
Tech. ● Bring hands down in front of Tanden
Ibuki ● Exhale

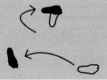

気を付け　礼　気を付け

立ち方●結び立ち
注意点●顎を引き、両手は真っすぐ
伸ばして大腿側部に付ける
Stance ● Musubidachi
Point ● Pull chin back. Keep
fingers straight and hands on
outer thight.

立ち方●結び立ち
注意点●前方30度位、礼は深すぎ
ない
Stance ● Musubidachi
Point ● Bow forward for 30° .Be
careful not to bow too deeply

立ち方●結び立ち
注意点●顎を引き、両手は真っすぐ
伸ばして大腿側部に付ける
Stance ● Musubidachi
Point ● Pull chin back. Keep
fingers straight and hands on
outer thight.

裏側

太極
掛け受け

タイキョクカケウケ1
Taikyoku
Kakeuke 1

型のポイント

　「太極掛け受け1」の「受け」は三戦立ちで転身し、「蹴り・当て」は前屈立ちで移動する。「太極掛け受け2」は「受け」を猫足立ち、「蹴り・当て」は前屈立ちで移動転身する。

　「太極掛け受け2」では「受け」の挙動動作は猫足立ちによる掛け受けを3連続動作（定位置から前進・後退）で行ってから、前蹴りからの前屈立ち肘当てで移動する。

　「受け」は掛け受け、「蹴り・当て」は前蹴り・中段肘当てで移動転身は素早く行う。

　「太極」とは移動転身する演武線を言い、スタート位置"用意"から"直れ"まで1〜30の挙動動作を演武する。

In Taikyoku Kakeuke 1, blocks are performed in Sanchin Dachi while kicks/strikes are performed in Zenkutsu Dachi. In Taikyoku Kakeuke 2, Kakeuke is performed in Nekoashi Dachi while kicks/strikes are performed in Zenkutsu Dachi. In Taikyoku Kakeuke 2, Kakeuke is performed in succession from Nekoashi Dachi (once in the original position, once stepping forward, and once stepping back) before performing Maegeri and moving into Zenkutsu Dachi with Hijiate.

All blocks are Kakeuke, all kicks are Maegeri, and all strikes are Chudan Hijiate. All steps in the kata are performed quickly.

The word "Taikyoku" means the direction of movement. There are 30 movements in Taikyoku Kakeuke, from "Heiko Dachi Yōi" at the starting position to "Naore."

気を付け	礼	気を付け

中間動作

裏側

立ち方●結び立ち
注意点●顎を引き、両手は真っすぐ
伸ばして大腿側部につける
Stance ● Musubidachi
Point ● Pull chin back. Keep
fingers straight and hands on
outer thight.

立ち方●結び立ち
注意点●前方30度位、礼は深すぎ
ない
Stance ● Musubidachi
Point ● Bow forward for 30°.Be
careful not to bow too deeply

立ち方●結び立ち
Stance ● Musubidachi

用意 1　　　用意 2　　　用意 3

裏側

立ち方●結び立ち
注意点●右掌内側、丹田の前で重ね
丹田集中
息吹●ゆっくり呑
Stance ● Musubidachi
Point ● Right hand on the
inside. Hands are crossed in
front of Tanden
Ibuki ● Inhale slowly

立ち方●平行立ち
注意点●爪先を支点に踵を外に開く
Stance ● Heiko Dachi
Point ● Keep balls of feet in
place and only move heels

立ち方●平行立ち
注意点●両拳は脇を締めながら体側
へ、正拳は真下へ向けて、両肩を落
とす
息吹●ゆっくり吐
Stance ● Heiko Dachi
Point ● Keep elbows against
side of body, fists pointing
straight down, and shoulders
relaxed
Ibuki ● Exhale slowly

第1挙動	第2挙動	第3挙動

中間動作

裏側

立ち方●左三戦立ち
技●左掛け受け
Stance ● Left Sanchin Dachi
Tech. ● Left Kakeuke

技●右前蹴り
Tech. ● Right Maegeri

立ち方●右前屈立ち
技●右中段肘当て
Stance ● Right Zenkutsu Dachi
Tech. ● Right Chudan Hijiate

第４挙動　　　　第５挙動　　　　第６挙動

立ち方●右三戦立ち
技●右掛け受け
Stance ● Right Sanchin Dachi
Tech. ● Right Kakeuke

技●左前蹴り
Tech. ● Left Maegeri

立ち方●左前屈立ち
技●左中段肘当て
Stance ● Left Zenkutsu Dachi
Tech. ● Left Chudan Hijiate

裏側

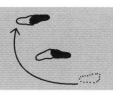

第7挙動	第8挙動	第9挙動

裏側

立ち方●左三戦立ち
技●左掛け受け
Stance ● Left Sanchin Dachi
Tech. ● Left Kakeuke

技●右前蹴り
Tech. ● Right Maegeri

立ち方●右前屈立ち
技●右中段肘当て
Stance ● Right Zenkutsu Dachi
Tech. ● Right Chudan Hijiate

第 10 挙動　　第 11 挙動　　第 12 挙動

裏側

技●左前蹴り
Tech. ● Left Maegeri

立ち方●左前屈立ち
技●左中段肘当て
Stance ● Left Zenkutsu Dachi
Tech. ● Left Chudan Hijiate

技●右前蹴り
Tech. ● Right Maegeri

第13挙動	第14挙動	第15挙動

中間動作

裏側

立ち方●右前屈立ち
技●右中段肘当て
注意点●気合
Stance ● Right Zenkutsu Dachi
Tech. ● Right Chudan Hijiate
Point ● Kiai

立ち方●左三戦立ち
技●左掛け受け
Stance ● Left Sanchin Dachi
Tech. ● Left Kakeuke

技●右前蹴り
Tech. ● Right Maegeri

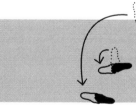

第 16 挙動　　　第 17 挙動　　　第 18 挙動

裏側

立ち方●右前屈立ち
技●右中段肘当て
Stance ● Right Zenkutsu Dachi
Tech. ● Right Chudan Hijiate

立ち方●右三戦立ち
技●右掛け受け
Stance ● Right Sanchin Dachi
Tech. ● Right Kakeuke

技●左前蹴り
Tech. ● Left Maegeri

第19挙動	第20挙動	第21挙動

中間動作

裏側

立ち方●左前屈立ち
技●左中段肘当て
Stance ● Left Zenkutsu Dachi
Tech. ● Left Chudan Hijiate

立ち方●左三戦立ち
技●左掛け受け
Stance ● Left Sanchin Dachi
Tech. ● Left Kakeuke

技●右前蹴り
Tech. ● Right Maegeri

第 22 挙動　　　第 23 挙動　　　第 24 挙動

立ち方●右前屈立ち
技●右中段肘当て
Stance ● Right Zenkutsu Dachi
Tech. ● Right Chudan Hijiate

技●左前蹴り
Tech. ● Left Maegeri

立ち方●左前屈立ち
技●左中段肘当て
Stance ● Left Zenkutsu Dachi
Tech. ● Left Chudan Hijiate

裏側

第25挙動	第26挙動	第27挙動

中間動作

裏側

技●右前蹴り
Tech. ● Right Maegeri

立ち方●右前屈立ち
技●右中段肘当て
注意点●気合
Stance ● Right Zenkutsu Dachi
Tech. ● Right Chudan Hijiate
Point ● Kiai

立ち方●左三戦立ち
技●左掛け受け
Stance ● Left Sanchin Dachi
Tech. ● Left Kakeuke

第 28 挙動	第 29 挙動	第 30 挙動

裏側

技●右前蹴り
Tech. ● Right Maegeri

立ち方●右前屈立ち
技●右中段肘当て
Stance ● Right Zenkutsu Dachi
Tech. ● Right Chudan Hijiate

立ち方●右三戦立ち
技●右掛け受け
注意点●受けはゆっくり
Stance ● Right Sanchin Dachi
Tech. ● Right Kakeuke
Point ● Block slowly

直って　　　　　　直って　　　　　気を付け

中間動作

裏側

立ち方●前足を引いて結び立ち
技●右手掌上に重ねる
息吹●呑
Stance ● Step back w/ right
foot into Musubidachi
Tech. ● Place right hand on top
of left
Ibuki ● Inhale

立ち方●結び立ち
技●手掌を摺り合わせて丹田集中
息吹●吐
Stance ● Musubidachi
Tech. ● Bring hands down in
front of Tanden
Ibuki ● Exhale

立ち方●結び立ち
注意点●顎を引き、両手は真っすぐ
伸ばして大腿側部に付ける
Stance ● Musubidachi
Point ● Pull chin back. Keep
fingers straight and hands on
outer thight.

礼　　　　　　　気を付け

立ち方●結び立ち
注意点●前方 30 度位、礼は深すぎない
Stance ● Musubidachi
Point ● Bow forward for 30°.Be careful not to bow too deeply

立ち方●結び立ち
注意点●顎を引き、両手は真っすぐ伸ばして大腿側部に付ける
Stance ● Musubidachi
Point ● Pull chin back. Keep fingers straight and hands on outer thight.

裏側

太極
廻し受け1

タイキョクマワシウケ1
Taikyoku
Mawashiuke 1

型のポイント

　「太極廻し受け1」の「受け」は三戦立ち、「肘当て4本動作」は四股立ち斜角で移動する。

　「太極廻し受け2」は「受け」を猫足立ちで転身し、「肘当て4本動作」は四股立ち斜角で移動する。「受け」は廻し受け、「肘当て4本動作」は横肘当て・裏打ち・下段払い・中段正拳突きで移動転身は素早く行う。

　「太極廻し受け2」「受け」の挙動動作は猫足立ちによる廻し受けを3連続動作（定位置から前進・後退）で転身し「肘当て4本動作」は四股立ち斜角で移動する。

　「太極」とは移動転身する演武線を言い、スタート位置"用意"から"直れ"まで1〜60の挙動動作を演武する。

In Taikyoku Mawashiuke 1, blocks are performed in Sanchin Dachi while Hijiate Yonhon Dōsa is performed in Shiko Dachi 45°.

In Taikyoku Mawashiuke 2, blocks are performed in Nekoashi Dachi while Hijiate Yonhon Dōsa is performed in Shiko Dachi 45°.

All blocks are Mawashiuke. And all strikes are Hijiate Yonhon Dōsa. Hijiate Yonhon Dōsa includes Yoko Hijiate, Urauchi, Gedan Barai, and Chudan Seiken Tsuki. All steps in the kata are performed quickly.

In Taikyoku Mawashiuke 2, Mawashiuke is performed in succession from Nekoashi Dachi (once in the original position, once stepping forward, and once stepping back) before performing Hijiate Yonhon Dōsa and moving into Shiko Dachi 45°.

The word "Taikyoku" means the direction of movement. There are 60 movements in Taikyoku Mawashiuke, from "Heiko Dachi Yōi" at the starting position to "Naore."

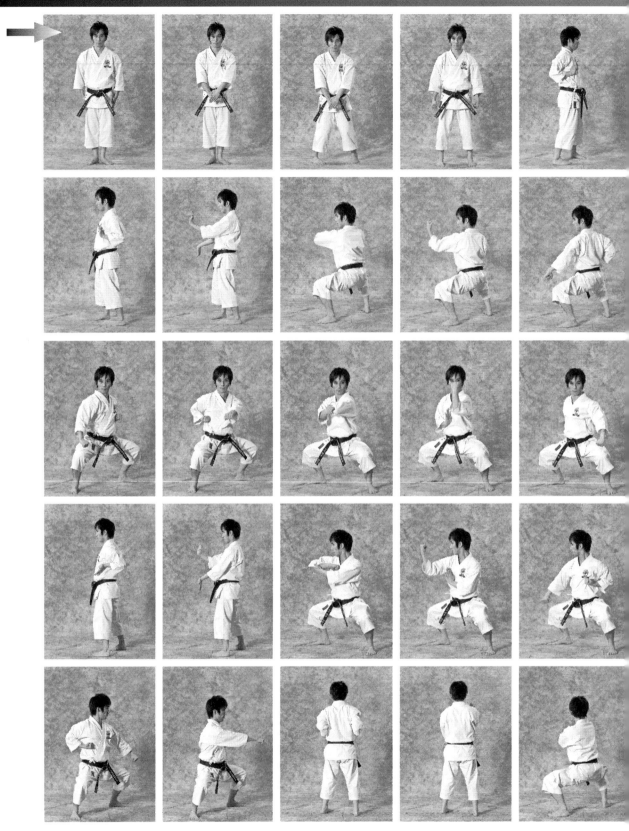

気を付け　　　　礼　　　　気を付け

裏側

立ち方●結び立ち
注意点●顎を引き、両手は真っすぐ
伸ばして大腿側部につける
Stance ● Musubidachi
Point ● Pull chin back. Keep
fingers straight and hands on
outer thight.

立ち方●結び立ち
注意点●前方 30 度位、礼は深すぎ
ない
Stance ● Musubidachi
Point ● Bow forward for 30° .Be
careful not to bow too deeply

立ち方●結び立ち
Stance ● Musubidachi

用意1	用意2	用意3

中間動作

裏側

立ち方●結び立ち
注意点●右掌内側、丹田の前で重ね
丹田集中
息吹●ゆっくり呑
Stance ● Musubidachi
Point ● Right hand on the
inside. Hands are crossed in
front of Tanden
Ibuki ● Inhale slowly

立ち方●平行立ち
注意点●爪先を支点に踵を外に開く
Stance ● Heiko Dachi
Point ● Keep balls of feet in
place and only move heels

立ち方●平行立ち
注意点●両拳は脇を締めながら体側
へ、正拳は真下へ向けて、両肩を落
とす
息吹●ゆっくり吐
Stance ● Heiko Dachi
Point ● Keep elbows against
side of body, fists pointing
straight down, and shoulders
relaxed
Ibuki ● Exhale slowly

第１挙動	第２挙動	第３挙動

		裏側

立ち方●左三戦立ち
技●右廻し受け
Stance ● Left Sanchin Dachi
Tech. ● Mawashiuke right hand
on top

立ち方●左三戦立ち
技●両手底掌当て
Stance ● Left Sanchin Dachi
Tech. ● Double arm Teisho Ate
(right hand on top)

立ち方●右四股立ち斜角
技●右横肘当て
Stance ● Right Shiko Dachi 45°
Tech. ● Right Yoko Hijiate

第４挙動	第５挙動	第６挙動

中間動作

裏側

立ち方●右四股立ち斜角	立ち方●右四股立ち斜角	立ち方●右四股立ち斜角
技●右裏打ち	技●右下段払い	技●左中段正拳突き
Stance ● Right Shiko Dachi 45°	Stance ● Right Shiko Dachi 45°	Stance ● Right Shiko Dachi 45°
Tech. ● Right Urauchi	Tech. ● Right Gedan Barai	Tech. ● Left Chudan Tsuki

第７挙動　　　第８挙動　　　第９挙動

裏側

立ち方●右三戦立ち
技●左廻し受け
Stance ● Right Sanchin Dachi
Tech. ● Mawashiuke left hand
on top

立ち方●右三戦立ち
技●両手底掌当て
Stance ● Right Sanchin Dachi
Tech. ● Double arm Teisho Ate
(left hand on top)

立ち方●左四股立ち斜角
技●左横肘当て
Stance ● Left Shiko Dachi 45°
Tech. ● Left Yoko Hijiate

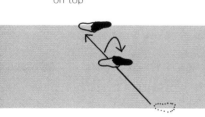 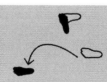

第 10 挙動	第 11 挙動	第 12 挙動

中間動作

裏側

立ち方●左四股立ち斜角
技●左裏打ち
Stance ● Left Shiko Dachi 45°
Tech. ● Left Urauchi

立ち方●左四股立ち斜角
技●左下段払い
Stance ● Left Shiko Dachi 45°
Tech. ● Left Gedan Barai

立ち方●左四股立ち斜角
技●右中段正拳突き
Stance ● Left Shiko Dachi 45°
Tech. ● Right Chudan Tsuki

第13挙動　　　第14挙動　　　第15挙動

裏側

立ち方●左三戦立ち
技●右廻し受け
Stance ● Left Sanchin Dachi
Tech. ● Mawashiuke right hand
on top

立ち方●左三戦立ち
技●両手底掌当て
Stance ● Left Sanchin Dachi
Tech. ● Double arm Teisho Ate
(right hand on top)

立ち方●右四股立ち斜角
技●右横肘当て
Stance ● Right Shiko Dachi 45°
Tech. ● Right Yoko Hijiate

第16挙動　第17挙動　第18挙動

中間動作

裏側

立ち方●右四股立ち斜角
技●右裏打ち
Stance ● Right Shiko Dachi 45°
Tech. ● Right Urauchi

立ち方●右四股立ち斜角
技●右下段払い
Stance ● Right Shiko Dachi 45°
Tech. ● Right Gedan Barai

立ち方●右四股立ち斜角
技●左中段正拳突き
Stance ● Right Shiko Dachi 45°
Tech. ● Left Chudan Tsuki

第19挙動　　　第20挙動　　　第21挙動

裏側

立ち方●左四股立ち斜角
技●左横肘当て
Stance ● Left Shiko Dachi 45°
Tech. ● Left Yoko Hijiate

立ち方●左四股立ち斜角
技●左裏打ち
Stance ● Left Shiko Dachi 45°
Tech. ● Left Urauchi

立ち方●左四股立ち斜角
技●左下段払い
Stance ● Left Shiko Dachi 45°
Tech. ● Left Gedan Barai

第22挙動　　　　第23挙動　　　　第24挙動

中間動作

裏側

立ち方●左四股立ち斜角
技●右中段正拳突き
Stance ● Left Shiko Dachi 45°
Tech. ● Right Chudan Tsuki

立ち方●右四股立ち斜角
技●右横肘当て
Stance ● Right Shiko Dachi 45°
Tech. ● Right Yoko Hijiate

立ち方●右四股立ち斜角
技●右裏打ち
Stance ● Right Shiko Dachi 45°
Tech. ● Right Urauchi

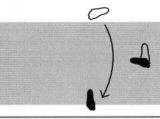

第25挙動	第26挙動	第27挙動

裏側

立ち方●右四股立ち斜角
技●右下段払い
Stance ● Right Shiko Dachi 45°
Tech. ● Right Gedan Barai

立ち方●右四股立ち斜角
技●左中段正拳突き
注意点●気合
Stance ● Right Shiko Dachi 45°
Tech. ● Left Chudan Tsuki
Point ● Kiai

立ち方●左三戦立ち
技●右廻し受け
Stance ● Left Sanchin Dachi
Tech. ● Mawashiuke right hand on top

第 28 挙動	第 29 挙動	第 30 挙動

中間動作

裏側

立ち方●左三戦立ち
技●両手底掌当て
Stance ● Left Sanchin Dachi
Tech. ● Double arm Teisho Ate
(right hand on top)

立ち方●右四股立ち斜角
技●右横肘当て
Stance ● Right Shiko Dachi 45°
Tech. ● Right Yoko Hijiate

立ち方●右四股立ち斜角
技●右裏打ち
Stance ● Right Shiko Dachi 45°
Tech. ● Right Urauchi

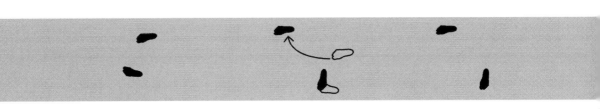

第31挙動	第32挙動	第33挙動

裏側

立ち方●右四股立ち斜角
技●右下段払い
Stance ● Right Shiko Dachi 45°
Tech. ● Right Gedan Barai

立ち方●右四股立ち斜角
技●左中段正拳突き
Stance ● Right Shiko Dachi 45°
Tech. ● Left Chudan Tsuki

立ち方●右三戦立ち
技●左廻し受け
Stance ● Right Sanchin Dachi
Tech. ● Mawashiuke left hand on top

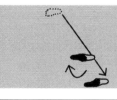

第 34 挙動	第 35 挙動	第 36 挙動

中間動作

裏側

立ち方●右三戦立ち
技●両手底掌当て
Stance ● Right Sanchin Dachi
Tech. ● Double arm Teisho Ate
(left hand on top)

立ち方●左四股立ち斜角
技●左横肘当て
Stance ● Left Shiko Dachi 45°
Tech. ● Left Yoko Hijiate

立ち方●左四股立ち斜角
技●左裏打ち
Stance ● Left Shiko Dachi 45°
Tech. ● Left Urauchi

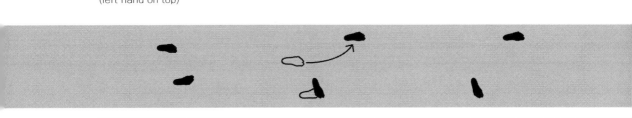

第37挙動　　　　第38挙動　　　　第39挙動

裏側

立ち方●左四股立ち斜角
技●左下段払い
Stance ● Left Shiko Dachi 45°
Tech. ● Left Gedan Barai

立ち方●左四股立ち斜角
技●右中段正拳突き
Stance ● Left Shiko Dachi 45°
Tech. ● Right Chudan Tsuki

立ち方●左三戦立ち
技●右廻し受け
Stance ● Left Sanchin Dachi
Tech. ● Mawashiuke right hand on top

第40挙動	第41挙動	第42挙動

中間動作

裏側

立ち方●左三戦立ち
技●両手底掌当て
Stance ● Left Sanchin Dachi
Tech. ● Double arm Teisho Ate
(right hand on top)

立ち方●右四股立ち斜角
技●右横肘当て
Stance ● Right Shiko Dachi 45°
Tech. ● Right Yoko Hijiate

立ち方●右四股立ち斜角
技●右裏打ち
Stance ● Right Shiko Dachi 45°
Tech. ● Right Urauchi

第 43 挙動　第 44 挙動　第 45 挙動

裏側

立ち方●右四股立ち斜角
技●右下段払い
Stance ● Right Shiko Dachi 45°
Tech. ● Right Gedan Barai

立ち方●右四股立ち斜角
技●左中段正拳突き
Stance ● Right Shiko Dachi 45°
Tech. ● Left Chudan Tsuki

立ち方●左四股立ち斜角
技●左横肘当て
Stance ● Left Shiko Dachi 45°
Tech. ● Left Yoko Hijiate

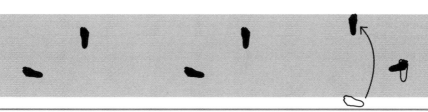

第 46 挙動	第 47 挙動	第 48 挙動

中間動作

裏側

立ち方●左四股立ち斜角
技●左裏打ち
Stance ● Left Shiko Dachi 45°
Tech. ● Left Urauchi

立ち方●左四股立ち斜角
技●左下段払い
Stance ● Left Shiko Dachi 45°
Tech. ● Left Gedan Barai

立ち方●左四股立ち斜角
技●右中段正拳突き
Stance ● Left Shiko Dachi 45°
Tech. ● Right Chudan Tsuki

第 49 挙動	第 50 挙動	第 51 挙動

立ち方●右四股立ち斜角
技●右横肘当て
Stance ● Right Shiko Dachi 45°
Tech. ● Right Yoko Hijiate

立ち方●右四股立ち斜角
技●右裏打ち
Stance ● Right Shiko Dachi 45°
Tech. ● Right Urauchi

立ち方●右四股立ち斜角
技●右下段払い
Stance ● Right Shiko Dachi 45°
Tech. ● Right Gedan Barai

裏側

第 52 挙動	第 53 挙動	第 54 挙動

中間動作

裏側

立ち方●右四股立ち斜角
技●左中段正拳突き
注意点●気合
Stance ● Right Shiko Dachi 45°
Tech. ● Left Chudan Tsuki
Point ● Kiai

立ち方●左三戦立ち
技●右廻し受け
Stance ● Left Sanchin Dachi
Tech. ● Mawashiuke right hand
on top

立ち方●左三戦立ち
技●両手底掌当て
Stance ● Left Sanchin Dachi
Tech. ● Double arm Teisho Ate
(right hand on top)

第 55 挙動　第 56 挙動　第 57 挙動

立ち方●右四股立ち斜角
技●右横肘当て

Stance ● Right Shiko Dachi 45°
Tech. ● Right Yoko Hijiate

立ち方●右四股立ち斜角
技●右裏打ち

Stance ● Right Shiko Dachi 45°
Tech. ● Right Urauchi

立ち方●右四股立ち斜角
技●右下段払い

Stance ● Right Shiko Dachi 45°
Tech. ● Right Gedan Barai

裏側

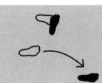

第58挙動　　　　第59挙動　　　　第60挙動

中間動作

裏側

立ち方●右四股立ち斜角
技●左中段正拳突き
Stance ● Right Shiko Dachi 45°
Tech. ● Left Chudan Tsuki

立ち方●右三戦立ち
技●左廻し受け
Stance ● Right Sanchin Dachi
Tech. ● Mawashiuke left hand
on top

立ち方●右三戦立ち
技●両手底掌当て
注意点●ゆっくりと
Stance ● Right Sanchin Dachi
Tech. ● Double arm Teisho Ate
(left hand on top)
Point ● Do slowly

直って	直って	気を付け

裏側

立ち方●前足を引いて結び立ち
技●右手掌上に重ねる
息吹●呑
Stance ● Step back w/ right foot into Musubidachi
Tech. ● Place right hand on top of left
Ibuki ● Inhale

立ち方●結び立ち
技●手掌を摺り合わせて丹田集中
息吹●吐
Stance ● Musubidachi
Tech. ● Bring hands down in front of Tanden
Ibuki ● Exhale

立ち方●結び立ち
注意点●顎を引き、両手は真っすぐ伸ばして大腿側部に付ける
Stance ● Musubidachi
Point ● Pull chin back. Keep fingers straight and hands on outer thight.

礼　　　気を付け

中間動作

裏側

立ち方●結び立ち
注意点●前方30度位、礼は深すぎ
ない
Stance ● Musubidachi
Point ● Bow forward for 30° .Be
careful not to bow too deeply

立ち方●結び立ち
注意点●顎を引き、両手は真っすぐ
伸ばして大腿側部に付ける
Stance ● Musubidachi
Point ● Pull chin back. Keep
fingers straight and hands on
outer thight.

裏側

ゲキサイ第1

撃砕第 1
Gekisai
Dai-ichi

型のポイント

　「ゲキサイ第1」と「ゲキサイ第2」は、流祖・宮城長順先生によって創案された初心者のための練習型で、全日本空手道剛柔会では「太極型」と共に"普及型"と呼ぶ。

　5種類の「太極型」を一つにしたのが「ゲキサイ第1・第2」である。

　「立ち方、受け、蹴り」が含まれる「ゲキサイ第1」に対して「ゲキサイ第2」は「猫足立ち」、「掛け受け、廻し受け」等が加わる。

　分解動作は、全日本空手道剛柔会が制定しているゲキサイ型分解組手 ゲキサイ第1（1本〜4本）、ゲキサイ第2（1本〜4本）の中から、ゲキサイ第1は一本目、二本目、三本目、四本目までの一部を、ゲキサイ第2は一本目、二本目、三本目までの一部を掲載している。

Gekisai Dai-ichi and Gekisai Dai-ni were created for beginners by Chojun Miyagi Sensei, the founder of Goju-ryu.
J.K.G.A. calls Gekisai and Taikyoku kata "Fukyu kata " (kata for propagation).
The two Gekisai kata were created by combining the techniques used in the five Taikyoku kata.
Gekisai Dai-ichi includes different stances, blocks, and kicks. Gekisai Dai-ni adds Nekoashi Dachi, Kakeuke, and Mawashiuke.
The Gekisai Dai-ichi Kata Bunkai created by J.K.G.A. contains 4 parts all together. Pictures taken from parts 1, 2, 3, and 4 are included in the following pages. The Gekisai Dai-ni Kata Bunkai contains 4 parts, Pictures taken from parts 1, 2, and 3 are included in this manual.

前屈立ち肘当て4本動作では、下段払いの際に引き手を使ってもよい。
When performing Gedan Barai in Zenkutsu Dachi Hijiate Yonhon Dōsa, Hikite may be used as shown in the photos.

気を付け	礼	気を付け

中間動作

裏側

立ち方●結び立ち
注意点●顎を引き、両手は真っすぐ
伸ばして大腿側部に付ける
Stance ● Musubidachi
Point ● Pull chin back. Keep
fingers straight and hands on
outer thight.

立ち方●結び立ち
注意点●前方30度位、礼は深すぎ
ない
Stance ● Musubidachi
Point ● Bow forward for 30° .Be
careful not to bow too deeply

立ち方●結び立ち
Stance ● Musubidachi

用意１　　　　用意２　　　　用意３

立ち方●結び立ち
注意点●右掌内側、丹田の前で重ね
丹田集中
息吹●ゆっくり呑
Stance ● Musubidachi
Point ● Right hand on the
inside. Hands are crossed in
front of Tanden
Ibuki ● Inhale slowly

立ち方●平行立ち
注意点●爪先を支点に踵を外に開く
Stance ● Heiko Dachi
Point ● Keep balls of feet in
place and only move heels

立ち方●平行立ち
注意点●両拳は脇を締めながら体側
へ、正拳は真下へ向けて、両肩を落
とす
息吹●ゆっくり吐
Stance ● Heiko Dachi
Point ● Keep elbows against
side of body, fists pointing
straight down, and shoulders
relaxed
Ibuki ● Exhale slowly

裏側

第１挙動	第２挙動	第３挙動

中間動作

裏側

立ち方●左三戦立ち
技●左上段受け
Stance ● Left Sanchin Dachi
Tech. ● Left Jodan Uke

立ち方●右三戦立ち
技●右中段正拳突き
Stance ● Right Sanchin Dachi
Tech. ● Right Chudan Tsuki

立ち方●四股立ち直角
技●左下段払い
注意点●前足を後退、目線はそのまま
Stance ● Shiko Dachi 90°
Tech. ● Left Gedan Barai
Point ● Move right foot back.
Eyes don't move

【分解】
Bunkai

一本目 No.1

第４挙動	第５挙動	第６挙動

立ち方●右三戦立ち
技●右上段受け
Stance ● Right Sanchin Dachi
Tech. ● Right Jodan Uke

立ち方●左三戦立ち
技●左中段正拳突き
Stance ● Left Sanchin Dachi
Tech. ● Left Chudan Tsuki

立ち方●四股立ち直角
注意点●前足を後退、目線はそのまま
Stance ● Shiko Dachi 90°
Tech. ● Right Gedan Barai
Point ● Move left foot back.
Eyes don't move

裏側

二本目 No.2

第７挙動	第８挙動	第９挙動

中間動作

裏側

立ち方●左三戦立ち
技●左中段受け
注意点●中段受けはゆっくり
Stance ● Left Sanchin Dachi
Tech. ● Left Chudan Uke
Point ● Block slowly

立ち方●右三戦立ち
技●右中段受け
注意点●一歩前進。受けはゆっくり
Stance ● Right Sanchin Dachi
Tech. ● Right Chudan Uke
Point ● Step forward. Block slowly

技●左前蹴り
Tech. ● Left Maegeri

裏側

立ち方●左前屈立ち
技●左中段肘当て
注意点●挙動 10 から 13 までは連
続動作
Stance ● Left Zenkutsu Dachi
Tech. ● Left Chudan Hijiate
Point ● Do 10-13 as one combination

立ち方●左前屈立ち
技●左上段裏打ち
Stance ● Left Zenkutsu Dachi
Tech. ● Left Jodan Urauchi

立ち方●左前屈立ち
技●左下段払い
Stance ● Left Zenkutsu Dachi
Tech. ● Left Gedan Barai

三本目　No.3

第13挙動	第14挙動	第15挙動

中間動作

裏側

立ち方●左前屈立ち 技●右中段正拳突き Stance ● Left Zenkutsu Dachi Tech. ● Right Chudan Tsuki	技●右足払い、右手開手旋回 注意点●足払いは素早く Tech. ● Right Ashibarai, Twist right hand toword body, and open hands Point ● Do Ashibarai quickly	立ち方●平行立ち 技●右手水平手刀打ち、左手開手 注意点●手刀は頸部を目標。気合 Stance ● Heiko Dachi Tech. ● Right Suihei Shuto Uchi, open hands Point ● Aim at opponent's neck. Kiai

【分解】
Bunkai

三本目（続き）

立ち方●左三戦立ち
技●左中段受け
注意点●後足を前進、受けはゆっくり
Stance ● Left Sanchin Dachi
Tech. ● Left Chudan Uke
Point ● Step forward w/ right foot. Block slowly

技●右前蹴り
Tech. ● Right Maegeri

立ち方●右前屈立ち
技●右中段肘当て
注意点●挙動 18 から 21 までは連続動作
Stance ● Right Zenkutsu Dachi
Tech. ● Right Chudan Hijiate
Point ● Do 18-21 as one combination

裏側

第19挙動	第20挙動	第21挙動

中間動作

裏側

立ち方●右前屈立ち
技●右上段裏打ち
Stance ● Right Zenkutsu Dachi
Tech. ● Right Jodan Urauchi

立ち方●右前屈立ち
技●右下段払い
Stance ● Right Zenkutsu Dachi
Tech. ● Right Gedan Barai

立ち方●左前屈立ち
技●左中段正拳突き
Stance ● Left Zenkutsu Dachi
Tech. ● Left Chudan Tsuki

第22挙動　　　第23挙動　　　第24挙動

技●左足払い、左手開手旋回
注意点●足払いは素早く
Tech. ● Left Ashibarai, Twist left hand towards body, and open hands
Point ● Do Ashibarai quickly

立ち方●平行立ち
技●左水平手刀打ち、右手開手
注意点●手刀は頸部を目標。気合
Stance ● Heiko Dachi
Tech. ● Left Suihei Shuto Uchi, open hands
Point ● Aim opponent's neck. Kiai

立ち方●右前屈立ち
技●右掛け受け、両手引き手
注意点●前足を斜め後方へ引く
Stance ● Right Zenkutsu Dachi
Tech. ● Right Kakeuke followed by double Hikite
Point ● Step back diagonally w/ left foot

裏側

四本目　No.4

第25挙動	第26挙動	第27挙動

中間動作

裏側

立ち方●右前屈立ち
技●両手突き
注意点●左上段正拳突き・右中段裏
突き。両手の拳は正中線
Stance ● Right Zenkutsu Dachi
Tech. ● Morote Tsuki
Point ● Left Jodan Tsuki and
right Chudan Urazuki. Fists are
in the center line of the body

立ち方●結び立ち
技●取り構え
注意点●右引き手・左中段伏せ。ゆっ
くり。左手は右引き手と同じ高さ
Stance ● Musubidachi
Tech. ● Tori kamae
Point ● Right Hikite and turn
left arm down at the same level.
Do slowly

立ち方●左前屈立ち
技●左掛け受け、両手引き手
注意点●右足を斜め後方へ引く
Stance ● Left Zenkutsu Dachi
Tech. ●Left Kakeuke followed
by doubleHikite
Point ● Step back diagonally w/
right foot

【分解】
Bunkai

四本目（続き）

第28挙動　　　直って　　　直って

立ち方●左前屈立ち
技●両手突き
注意点●右上段正拳突き・左中段裏突き。両手の拳は正中線
Stance ● Left Zenkutsu Dachi
Tech. ● Morote Tsuki
Point ● Right Jodan Tsuki and left ChudanUrazuki. Fists are in the center line of the body

立ち方●結び立ち
注意点●右手掌を上に重ねる。後足を前足に揃えて直る
息吹●呑
Stance ● Musubidachi
Tech. ● Step right foot forward into Musubidachi. Place right hand on top of left
Ibuki ● Inhale

立ち方●結び立ち
注意点●手掌を摺り合わせ、丹田集中
息吹●吐
Stance ● Musubidachi
Tech. ● Bring hands down in front of Tanden
Ibuki ● Exhale

裏側

気を付け	礼	気を付け

中間動作

裏側

立ち方●結び立ち
注意点●顎を引き、両手は真っすぐ
伸ばして大腿側部に付ける
Stance ● Musubidachi
Point ● Pull chin back. Keep
fingers straight and hands on
outer thight.

立ち方●結び立ち
注意点●前方30度位、礼は深すぎ
ない
Stance ● Musubidachi
Point ● Bow forward for 30° .Be
careful not to bow too deeply

立ち方●結び立ち
注意点●顎を引き、両手は真っすぐ
伸ばして大腿側部に付ける
Stance ● Musubidachi
Point ● Pull chin back. Keep
fingers straight and hands on
outer thight.

ゲキサイ第2

撃砕第 2
Gekisai Dai-ni

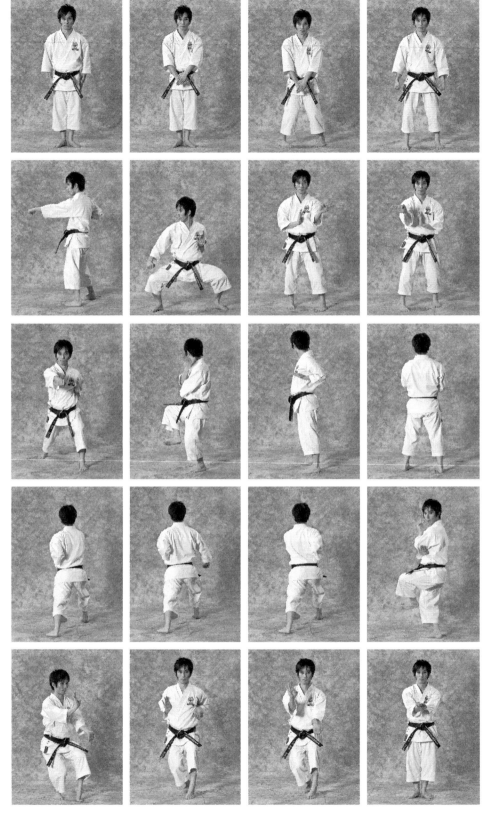

気を付け	礼	気を付け

中間動作

裏側

立ち方●結び立ち
注意点●顎を引き、両手は真っすぐ
伸ばして大腿側部につける
Stance ● Musubidachi
Point ● Pull chin back. Keep
fingers straight and hands on
outer thight.

立ち方●結び立ち
注意点●前方30度位、礼は深すぎ
ない
Stance ● Musubidachi
Point ● Bow forward for 30° .Be
careful not to bow too deeply

立ち方●結び立ち
Stance ● Musubidachi

用意1

用意2

用意3

裏側

立ち方●結び立ち
注意点●右掌内側、丹田の前で重ね
丹田集中
息吹●ゆっくり呑
Stance ● Musubidachi
Point ● Right hand on the
inside. Hands are crossed in
front of Tanden
Ibuki ● Inhale slowly

立ち方●平行立ち
注意点●爪先を支点に踵を外に開く
Stance ● Heiko Dachi
Point ● Keep balls of feet in
place and only move heels

立ち方●平行立ち
注意点●両拳は脇を締めながら体側
へ、正拳は真下へ向けて、両肩を落
とす
息吹●ゆっくり吐
Stance ● Heiko Dachi
Point ● Keep elbows against
side of body, fists pointing
straight down, and shoulders
relaxed
Ibuki ● Exhale slowly

	第１挙動	第２挙動	第３挙動

中間動作

裏側

立ち方●左三戦立ち
技●左上段受け
Stance ● Left Sanchin Dachi
Tech. ● Left Jodan Uke

立ち方●右三戦立ち
技●右中段正拳突き
Stance ● Right Sanchin Dachi
Tech. ● Right Seiken Tsuki

立ち方●四股立ち直角
技●左下段払い
注意点●前足を後退、目線はそのまま
Stance ● Shiko Dachi 90°
Tech. ● Left Gedan Barai
Point ● Move right foot back.
Eyes don't move

【分解】
Bunkai

一本目 No.1

第４挙動	第５挙動	第６挙動

裏側

立ち方●右三戦立ち
技●右上段受け
Stance ● Right Sanchin Dachi
Tech. ● Right Jodan Uke

立ち方●左三戦立ち
技●左中段正拳突き
Stance ● Left Sanchin Dachi
Tech. ● Left Chudan Tsuki

立ち方●四股立ち直角
技●右下段払い
注意点●前足を後退、目線はそのまま
Stance ● Shiko Dachi 90°
Tech. ● Right Gedan Barai
Point ● Move left foot back.
Eyes don't move

本目 No.2

第7挙動	第8挙動	第9挙動

中間動作

裏側

立ち方●左三戦立ち
技●左中段掛け受け
注意点●掛け受けはゆっくり
Stance ● Left Sanchin Dachi
Tech. ● Left Chudan Kakeuke
Point ● Block slowly

立ち方●右三戦立ち
技●右中段掛け受け
注意点●前進。掛け受けはゆっくり
Stance ● Right Sanchin Dachi
Tech. ● Right Chudan Kakeuke
Point ● Step forward. Block
slowly

技●左前蹴り
Tech. ● Left Maegeri

第10挙動　　　　第11挙動　　　　第12挙動

裏側

立ち方●左前屈立ち
技●左中段肘当て
注意点●挙動10から13までは連続動作
Stance ● Left Zenkutsu Dachi
Tech. ● Left Chudan Hijiate
Point ● Do 10-13 as one combination

立ち方●左前屈立ち
技●左上段裏打ち
Stance ● Left Zenkutsu Dachi
Tech. ● Left Jodan Urauchi

立ち方●左前屈立ち
技●左下段払い
Stance ● Left Zenkutsu Dachi
Tech. ● Left Gedan Barai

第13挙動　　　第14挙動　　　第15挙動

中間動作

裏側

立ち方●左前屈立ち
技●右中段正拳突き
Stance ● Left Zenkutsu Dachi
Tech. ● Right Chudan Tsuki

技●右足払い、右手開手旋回
注意点●足払いは素早く
Tech. ● Right Ashibarai, Twist right hand towards body, and open hands
Point ● Do Ashibarai quickly

立ち方●平行立ち
技●右水平手刀打ち、左手開手
注意点●手刀は頸部を目標。気合
Stance ● Heiko Dachi
Tech. ● Right Suihei Shuto Uchi, open hands
Point ● Aim at opponent's neck. Kiai

第16挙動　　第17挙動　　第18挙動

裏側

立ち方●左三戦立ち
技●左中段掛け受け
注意点●後足を前進、受けはゆっくり
Stance ● Left Sanchin Dachi
Tech. ● Left Chudan Kakeuke
Point ● Step foward w/ left foot.
Block slowly

立ち方●右三戦立ち
技●右中段掛け受け
注意点●後足を前進、受けはゆっくり
Stance ● Right Sanchin Dachi
Tech. ● Right Chudan Kakeuke
Point ● Step forward w/ right
foot. Block slowly

立ち方●左三戦立ち
技●左中段掛け受け
注意点●前足を後退、受けはゆっくり
Stance ● Left Sanchin Dachi
Tech. ● Left Chudan Kakeuke
Point ● Step back w/ right foot.
Block slowly

三本目　No.3

第 19 挙動	第 20 挙動	第 21 挙動

中間動作

裏側

技●右前蹴り
Tech. ● Right Maegeri

立ち方●右前屈立ち
技●右中段肘当て
注意点●挙動20から23までは連続動作
Stance ● Right Zenkutsu Dachi
Tech. ● Right Chudan Hijiate
Point ● Do 20-23 continuously

立ち方●右前屈立ち
技●右上段裏打ち
Stance ● Right Zenkutsu Dachi
Tech. ● Right Jodan Urauchi

【分解】
Bunkai

三本目（続き）

第22挙動　　　　　　　　第23挙動　　　　　　　　第24挙動

裏側

立ち方●右前屈立ち
技●右下段払い
Stance ● Right Zenkutsu Dachi
Tech. ● Right Gedan Barai

立ち方●右前屈立ち
技●左中段正拳突き
Stance ● Right Zenkutsu Dachi
Tech. ● Left Chudan Tsuki

技●左足払い、左手開手旋回
注意点●足払いは素早く
Tech. ● Left Ashibarai, Turn left
hand over, and open hands
Point ● Do Ashibarai quickly

中間動作

裏側

立ち方●平行立ち
技●左水平手刀打ち
注意点●手刀は頸部を目標。気合
Stance ● Heiko Dachi
Tech. ● Left Suihei Shuto Uchi,
open hands
Point ● Aim opponent's neck.
Kiai

立ち方●右猫足立ち
技●左廻し受け、両手引き手
注意点●前足を斜め後方へ引く
Stance ● Right Nekoashi dachi
Tech. ● Mawashiuke left hand
on top, and double arm Hikite
Point ● Step back diagonally w/
left foot

立ち方●右猫足立ち
技●両手底掌当て
注意点●左手鎖骨・右手鼠径部（そ
けいぶ）、両手底掌突きはゆっくり
Stance ● Right Nekoashi dachi
Tech. ● Teisho Ate
Point ● Do Teisho Ate slowly :
left hand to the collarbone, right
hand to the groin

【分解】
Bunkai

三本目（続き）

第28挙動	第29挙動	第30挙動

裏側

立ち方●左猫足立ち
技●右廻し受け、両手引き手
注意点●右足を斜め後方へ引く
Stance ● Left Nekoashi dachi
Tech. ● Mawashiuke right hand
on top and double arm Hikite
Point ● Step back diagonall w/
right foot

立ち方●左猫足立ち
技●両手底掌当て
注意点●右手鎖骨・左手鼠径部（そ
けいぶ）、両手底掌突きはゆっくり
Stance ● Left Nekoashi dachi
Tech. ● Teisho Ate
Point ● Do Teisho Ate slowly :
right hand to the collarbone, left
hand to the groin

立ち方●左猫足立ち
技●両手引き手
注意点●前足を正面に向け、両手を
引く
Stance ● Left Nekoashi dachi
Tech. ● Double arm Hikite
Point ● Move left foot toward
the front. Pull arms back

第31挙動　　　直って　　　直って

中間動作

裏側

立ち方●左猫足立ち
技●両手底掌当て
注意点●右手鎖骨・左手鼠径部（そけいぶ）。両手底掌突きはゆっくり
Stance ● Left Nekoashi dachi
Tech. ● Teisho Ate
Point ● Do Teisho Ate slowly : right hand to the collarbone, left hand to the groin

立ち方●前足を引いて結び立ち
技●右手掌上に重ねる
息吹●呑
Stance ● Step back w/ left foot into Musubidachi
Tech. ● Place right hand on top of left
Ibuki ● Inhale

立ち方●結び立ち
技●手掌を摺り合わせて丹田集中
息吹●吐
Stance ● Musubidachi
Tech. ● Bring hands down in front of Tanden
Ibuki ● Exhale

気を付け	礼	気を付け

裏側

立ち方●結び立ち
注意点●顎を引き、両手は真っすぐ伸ばして大腿側部に付ける
Stance ● Musubidachi
Point ● Pull chin back. Keep fingers straight and hands on outer thight.

立ち方●結び立ち
注意点●前方 30 度位、礼は深すぎない
Stance ● Musubidachi
Point ● Bow forward for 30° .Be careful not to bow too deeply

立ち方●結び立ち
注意点●顎を引き、両手は真っすぐ伸ばして大腿側部に付ける
Stance ● Musubidachi
Point ● Pull chin back. Keep fingers straight and hands on outer thight.

サイファー

砕破
Saifa

型のポイント

剛柔流「開手型」一番目の型である。

型としては一番短く、挙動数も少ない。型演武で最も大切な姿勢、目線の維持を異なる「立ち方」で修練し、剛柔流に独特な接近戦に用いる腰の使い方、スナップによる手技、足技が多い。一見容易に見えるが、難度の高い型と言える。サイファーの反復練習は更なる上級型のために欠かせない。

分解動作は、全日本空手道剛柔会が制定しているサイファー型分解組手（１本〜４本）から、一本目、二本目、三本目、四本目までの一部を掲載している。

This is the first kata of Goju-ryu's "Kaishu kata."

It is the shortest kata and has the fewest movements.

When practicing kata the most important point is to keep correct posture and direction of sight. In Saifa, these can be practiced in many different stances.

It also includes original Goju-ryu techniques for infighting such as proper use of hips, and snapping techniques with hands and feet.

Though it may look easy at first sight, it can be considered a more high level kata.

It is necessary to practice Saifa repeatedly before moving on to learn higher level kata.

The Saifa Kata Bunkai created by the J.K.G.A. contains 4 parts all together. Pictures taken from 1, 2, 3, and 4 are included in the following pages.

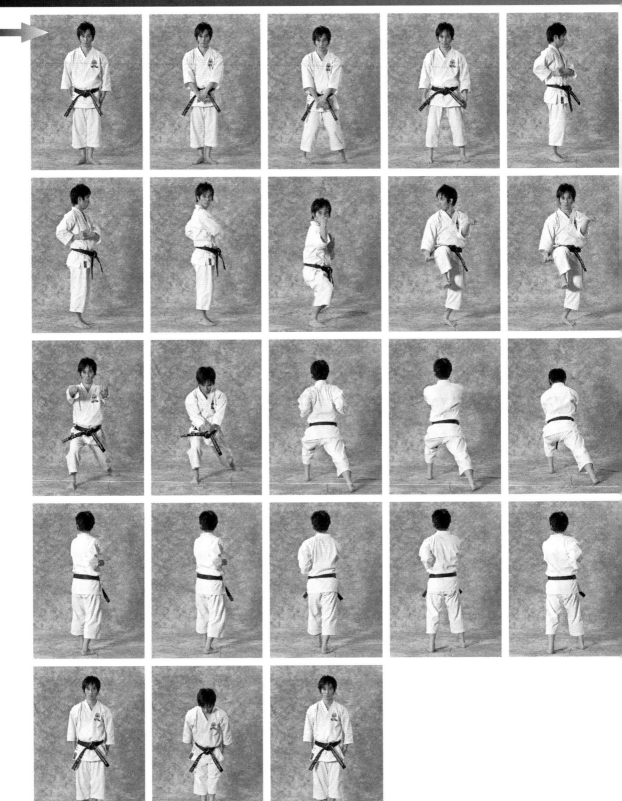

気を付け	礼	気を付け

中間動作

裏側

立ち方●結び立ち
注意点●顎を引き、両手は真っすぐ
伸ばして大腿側部につける
Stance ● Musubidachi
Point ● Pull chin back. Keep
fingers straight and hands on
outer thight.

立ち方●結び立ち
注意点●前方30度位、礼は深すぎ
ない
Stance ● Musubidachi
Point ● Bow forward for 30° .Be
careful not to bow too deeply

立ち方●結び立ち
Stance ● Musubidachi

用意1　　　　　　用意2　　　　　　用意3

裏側

立ち方●結び立ち
注意点●右掌内側、丹田の前で重ね
丹田集中
息吹●ゆっくり呑
Stance ● Musubidachi
Point ● Right hand on the
inside. Hands are crossed in
front of Tanden
Ibuki ● Inhale slowly

立ち方●平行立ち
注意点●爪先を支点に踵を外に開く
Stance ● Heiko Dachi
Point ● Keep balls of feet in
place and only move heels

立ち方●平行立ち
注意点●両拳は脇を締めながら体側
へ、正拳は真下へ向けて、両肩を落
とす
息吹●ゆっくり吐
Stance ● Heiko Dachi
Point ● Keep elbows against
side of body, fists pointing
straight down, and shoulders
relaxed
Ibuki ● Exhale slowly

第１挙動	第２挙動	第３挙動

裏側

立ち方●結び立ち
技●右引き手縦拳に左手掌を合わせる
注意点●右45度に前進
Stance ● Musubidachi
Tech. ● Put left palm on Right Hikite
Point ● Step forward right 45°

立ち方●結び立ち
技●引き手右拳を左へ捻り取る
注意点●外しは素早く、目線と同時
Stance ● Musubidachi
Tech. ● Bring right hand across body while twisting fist
Point ● Move quickly and simultaeously turn head forward

立ち方●右四股立ち直角
技●左底掌受け、右上段裏打ち
注意点●左足を引き、四股立ちと同時に打つ
Stance ● Right Shiko Dachi 90°
Tech. ● Left Teisho Uke, right Jodan Urauchi
Point ● Pull left foot back. Do Urauchi and make Shiko Dachi at the same time.

【分解】
Bunkai

一本目 No.1

第４挙動   第５挙動   第６挙動

裏側

立ち方●結び立ち
技●左引き手縦拳に右手掌を合わせる
注意点●左45度に前進
Stance ● Musubidachi
Tech. ● Put right palm on Left Hikite
Point ● Step forward right 45°

立ち方●結び立ち
技●引き手縦拳を右へ捻り取る
注意点●外しは素早く、目線と同時
Stance ● Musubidachi
Tech. ● Bring left hand across body while twisting fist
Point ● Move quickly and simultaeously turn head forward

立ち方●左四股立ち直角
技●右底掌受け、左上段裏打ち
注意点●右足を引き、四股立ちと同時に打つ
Stance ● Left Shiko Dachi 90°
Tech. ● Right Teisho Uke, left Jodan Urauchi
Point ● Pull right foot back. Do Urauchi and make Shiko Dachi at the same time.

第7挙動　　　第8挙動　　　第9挙動

裏側

立ち方●結び立ち
技●右引き手縦拳に左手掌を合わせる
注意点●右45度に前進
Stance ● Musubidachi
Tech. ● Put left palm on Right Hikite
Point ● Step forward right 45°

立ち方●結び立ち
技●引き手右拳を左へ捻り取る
注意点●外しは素早く、目線と同時
Stance ● Musubidachi
Tech. ● Bring right hand across body while twisting fist
Point ● Move quickly and simultaeously turn head forward

立ち方●右四股立ち直角
技●左底掌受け、右上段裏打ち
注意点●左足を引き、四股立ちと同時に打つ
Stance ● Right Shiko Dachi 90°
Tech. ● Left Teisho Uke, right Jodan Urauchi
Point ● Pull left foot back. Do Urauchi and make Shiko Dachi at the same time.

第10挙動　　　　　第11挙動　　　　　第12挙動

裏側

立ち方●左鷺足立ち
技●上下掬い受け
注意点●目線は西
Stance ● Left Sagiashi dachi
Tech. ● Sukuiuke left hand top
Point ● Look west

立ち方●左鷺足立ち
注意点●目線を南に向ける。膝当て
をする様にかい込む
Stance ● Left Sagiashi dachi
Point ● Look south. Raise knee
like Hiza Ate

技●右前蹴り
Tech. ● Right Maegeri

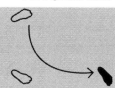

二本目　No.2

第13挙動　　　第14挙動　　　第15挙動

裏側

立ち方●右鷺足立ち
技●上下掬い受け
注意点●目線は東
Stance ● Right Sagiashi dachi
Tech. ● Sukuiuke right hand top
Point ● Look east

立ち方●右鷺足立ち
注意点●目線を南に向ける。膝当て
をする様にかい込む
Stance ● Right Sagiashi dachi
Point ● Look south. Raise knee
like Hiza Ate

技●左前蹴り
Tech. ● Left Maegeri

第16挙動　　　第17挙動　　　第18挙動

裏側

立ち方●右前屈立ち
技●両手交差取り
注意点●右手上交差引き取る
Stance ● Right Zenkutsu Dachi
Tech. ● Cross arms and pull
back
Point ● Place right hand on top
of left

立ち方●右前屈立ち
技●両手突き
Stance ● Right Zenkutsu Dachi
Tech. ● Double arm Tsuki

立ち方●右前屈立ち
技●右鉄槌当て
注意点●右膝は深め、左手開手、目
線は鉄槌の方向
Stance ● Right Zenkutsu Dachi
Tech. ● Right Tettsui Ate
Point ● Bend right knee more
deeply, open left hand and look
toward Tettsui.

第 19 挙動	第 20 挙動	第 21 挙動

裏側

立ち方●左前屈立ち
技●両手交差取り
注意点●前足を左に移動、後ろに回転、右手上交差引き取る
Stance ● Left Zenkutsu Dachi
Tech. ● Cross arms and pull back
Point ● Front leg moves left. Turn 180°. Right hand on top of left hand and pull back

立ち方●左前屈立ち
技●両手突き
Stance ● Left Zenkutsu Dachi
Tech. ● Double arm Tsuki

立ち方●左前屈立ち
技●左鉄槌当て
注意点●左膝は深め、右手開手、目線は鉄槌方向
Stance ● Left Zenkutsu Dachi
Tech. ● Left Tettsui Ate
Point ● Bend left knee more deeply, open right hand and look Tettsui.

【分解】
Bunkai

三本目 No.3

第22挙動　　　　第23挙動　　　　第24挙動

裏側

技●右足払い
注意点●右拳振り上げ
Tech. ● Right Ashibarai
Point ● Circle right fist over
head

立ち方●右レの字立ち
技●右上段鉄槌打ち
注意点●足払い・鉄槌は素早く。気合
Stance ● Right Renoji dachi
Tech.●Right Jodan Tettsui Uchi
Point ● Do Ashibarai and
Tettsui quickly. Kiai

立ち方●右レの字立ち
技●右開手、髪取り
Stance ● Right Renoji dachi
Tech. ● Open right hand and
grab hair

第 25 挙動	第 26 挙動	第 27 挙動

中間動作

裏側

立ち方●右レの字立ち
技●左下突き
注意点●右上段鉄槌と髪取り、下突きは連続
Stance ● Right Renoji dachi
Tech. ● Left Shita Zuki
Point ● Do right Jodan Tettsui, Kami Tori, and Shita Zuki as one combination

技●左足払い
注意点●左拳振り上げ
Tech. ● Left Ashibarai
Point ● Circle left fist over head

立ち方●左レの字立ち
技●左上段鉄槌打ち
注意点●足払い・鉄槌は素早く。気合
Stance ● Left Renoji dachi
Tech. ● Left Jodan Tettsui Uchi
Point ● Do quickly. Kiai

【分解】
Bunkai

四本目 No.4

第28挙動	第29挙動	第30挙動

立ち方●左レの字立ち
技●左開手、髪取り
Stance ● Left Renoji dachi
Tech. ● Open left hand and grab hair

立ち方●左レの字立ち
技●右下突き
注意点●左上段鉄槌と髪取り、下突きは連続
Stance ● Left Renoji dachi
Tech. ● Right Shita Zuki
Point ● Do 27-29 as one combination

立ち方●右三戦立ち
技●右手捻り返し
注意点●後足を前進と同時に右拳を捻り返す
Stance ● Right Sanchin dach
Tech. ● Turn right hand over
Point ● Step forward w/ right foot at the same time

第31挙動

第32挙動

中間動作

裏側

立ち方●右三戦立ち
技●左中段正拳突き
Stance ● Right Sanchin Dachi
Tech. ● Left Chudan Tsuki

立ち方●右猫足立ち
技●右中段背刀打ち
注意点●左手は開手の引き手
Stance ● Right Nekoashi dachi
Tech. ● Right Chudan Haito Uchi
Point ● Left hand is open Hikite

【分解】
Bunkai

別角度

四本目（続き）

第33挙動　　　第34挙動　　　直って

裏側

立ち方●右猫足立ち
技●左廻し受け
Stance ● Right Nekoashi dachi
Tech. ● Mawashiuke left hand
on top (slowly)

立ち方●右猫足立ち
技●両手底掌当て
注意点●廻し受け、両手底掌当ては
ゆっくり
Stance ● Right Nekoashi dachi
Tech. ● Double arm Teisho Ate
Point ● Do slowly

立ち方●前足を引いて結び立ち
技●右手掌上に重ねる
息吹●呑
Stance ● Step back w/ right
foot into Musubidachi
Tech. ● Place right hand on top
of left
Ibuki ● Inhale

直って	気を付け	礼

中間動作

裏側

立ち方●結び立ち
技●手掌を摺り合わせて丹田集中
息吹●吐
Stance ● Musubidachi
Tech. ● Bring hands down in front of Tanden
Ibuki ● Exhale

立ち方●結び立ち
注意点●顎を引き、両手は真っすぐ伸ばして大腿側部に付ける
Stance ● Musubidachi
Point ● Pull chin back. Keep fingers straight and hands on outer thight.

立ち方●結び立ち
注意点●前方30度位、礼は深すぎない
Stance ● Musubidachi
Point ● Bow forward for 30°.Be careful not to bow too deeply

気を付け

立ち方●結び立ち
注意点●顎を引き、両手は真っすぐ
伸ばして大腿側部につける
Stance ● Musubidachi
Point ● Pull chin back. Keep
fingers straight and hands on
outer thight.

セインチン

制引鎮
Seinchin

型のポイント

　唯一、蹴りの無い型であるが、「虎の型」とも言われる様に重心を落とした「四股立ち」での転身が多く、安定した斜角での移動と速い直角での攻防、柔らかな四股立ち転身は型の緩急を対称させる。

　演武線は南西・南東に対してと、北東・北西に対して対称させているので大変バランスの良い型である。

　分解動作は、全日本空手道剛柔会が制定しているセインチン型分解組手（１本〜４本）から、一本目、二本目、三本目、四本目までの一部を掲載している。

Seinchin is the only kata which does not include kicking. It is called "Tora no kata" (Tiger's kata) because of the many transitions in Shiko Dachi that are done while keeping a low center of gravity.

It has parts which contrast with each other. For example, the first part of the kata involves stepping forward slowly in Shiko Dachi 45° while another part involves moving quickly into Shiko Dachi 90°. Also, the smooth movements in Shiko Dachi, both quick and slow, help to create the pace while performing the kata.

It can be considered a balanced kata because the steps are symmetrical in four directions (southwest, southeast, northeast, and northwest).

The Seinchin Kata Bunkai created by the J.K.G.A. contains 4 parts all together. Pictures taken from 1, 2, 3, and 4 are included in following pages.

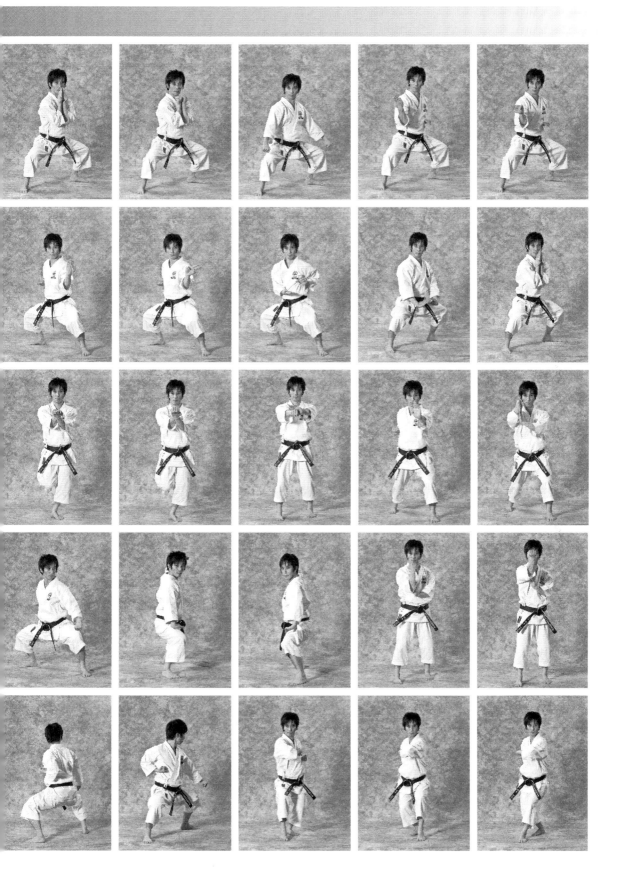

気を付け　　　　　　　礼　　　　　　　気を付け

裏側

立ち方●結び立ち
注意点●顎を引き、両手は真っすぐ
伸ばして大腿側部につける
Stance ● Musubidachi
Point ● Pull chin back. Keep
fingers straight and hands on
outer thight.

立ち方●結び立ち
注意点●前方30度位、礼は深すぎ
ない
Stance ● Musubidachi
Point ● Bow forward for 30° .Be
careful not to bow too deeply

立ち方●結び立ち
Stance ● Musubidachi

用意1	用意2	用意3

中間動作

裏側

立ち方●結び立ち
注意点●右掌内側、丹田の前で重ね
丹田集中
息吹●ゆっくり呑
Stance ● Musubidachi
Point ● Right hand on the
inside. Hands are crossed in
front of Tanden
Ibuki ● Inhale slowly

立ち方●平行立ち
注意点●爪先を支点に踵を外に開く
Stance ● Heiko Dachi
Point ● Keep balls of feet in
place and only move heels

立ち方●平行立ち
注意点●両拳は脇を締めながら体側
へ、正拳は真下へ向けて、両肩を落
とす
息吹●ゆっくり吐
Stance ● Heiko Dachi
Point ● Keep elbows against
side of body, fists pointing
straight down, and shoulders
relaxed
Ibuki ● Exhale slowly

第１挙動　　　第２挙動　　　第３挙動

裏側

立ち方●右四股立ち斜角
技●丹田前に八字構え
注意点●丸いボールを押さえるように丹田集中

Stance ● Right Shiko Dachi 45°
Tech. ● Hachiji kamae in front of Tanden
Point ● Position hands as if holding down a round ball and focus on Tanden

立ち方●右四股立ち斜角
技●両手背手合わせ
注意点●脇と肘を締め、指先は口割り

Stance ● Right Shiko Dachi 45°
Tech. ● Bring the backs of hands together
Point ● Bring fingers to mouth height. Break grab by twisting rms.

立ち方●右四股立ち斜角
技●両拳を握る
Stance ● Right Shiko Dachi 45°
Tech. ● Make fists

一本目 No.1

第4挙動	第5挙動	第6挙動

中間動作

裏側

立ち方●右四股立ち斜角
技●両手払い受け
Stance ● Right Shiko Dachi 45°
Tech. ● Double arm Harai Uke

立ち方●右四股立ち斜角
技●右開手中段受け、左手引き手（手掌が上）
Stance ● Right Shiko Dachi 45°
Tech. ● Right Chudan Uke open hand, Left Hikite

立ち方●右四股立ち斜角
技●右掛け受け
Stance ● Right Shiko Dachi 45°
Tech. ● Right Kakeuke

【分解】
Bunkai

一本目（続き）

第7挙動　　　第8挙動　　　第9挙動

裏側

立ち方●右四股立ち斜角
技●右掛取り、左貫手
注意点●掛取りは脇まで引き、手掌
が下。左貫手は斜め前膝方向、肘は
身体に密着
Stance ● Right Shiko Dachi 45°
Tech. ● Right Kake Tori, left
Nukite
Point ● Pull right hand back
towards underarm, Nukite in the
same direction as front knee.
Keep left elbow against the body

立ち方●左四股立ち斜角
技●丹田前に八字構え
注意点●丸いボールを押さえるように
丹田集中
Stance ● Left Shiko Dachi 45°
Tech. ● Hachiji kamae in front
of Tanden
Point ● Position hands as if
holding down a round ball and
focus on Tanden

立ち方●左四股立ち斜角
技●両手背手合わせ
注意点●脇と肘を締め、指先は口割り
Stance ● Left Shiko Dachi 45°
Tech. ● Bring the backs of
hands together
Point ● Bring fingers to mouth
height. Break grab by twisting
rms.

第10挙動	第11挙動	第12挙動

中間動作

裏側

立ち方●左四股立ち斜角
技●両拳を握る
Stance ● Left Shiko Dachi 45°
Tech. ● Make fists

立ち方●左四股立ち斜角
技●両手払い受け
Stance ● Left Shiko Dachi 45°
Tech. ● Double arm Harai Uke

立ち方●左四股立ち斜角
技●左開手中段受け、右手引き手（手
掌が上）
Stance ● Left Shiko Dachi 45°
Tech. ● Left Chudan Uke open
hand, Right Hikite

第 13 挙動 第 14 挙動 第 15 挙動

裏側

立ち方●左四股立ち斜角
技●左掛取り、右貫手
注意点●掛取りは脇まで引き、手掌が下。右貫手は斜め前膝方向、肘は身体に密着
Stance ● Left Shiko Dachi 45°
Tech. ● Keft Kake Tori, right Nukite
Point ● Pull right hand back towards underarm, Nukite in the same direction as front knee. Keep left elbow against the body

立ち方●右四股立ち斜角
技●丹田前に八字構え
注意点●丸いボールを押さえるように丹田集中
Stance ● Right Shiko Dachi 45°
Tech. ● Hachiji kamae in front of Tanden
Point ● Position hands as if holding down a round ball and focus on Tanden

立ち方●左四股立ち斜角
技●左掛け受け
Stance ● Left Shiko Dachi 45°
Tech. ● Left Kakeuke

第 16 挙動	第 17 挙動	第 18 挙動

中間動作

裏側

立ち方●右四股立ち斜角
技●両手背手合わせ
注意点●脇と肘を締め、指先は口割り
Stance ● Right Shiko Dachi 45°
Tech. ● Bring the backs of hands together
Point ● Bring fingers to mouth height. Break grab by twisting rms.

立ち方●右四股立ち斜角
技●両拳を握る
Stance ● Right Shiko Dachi 45°
Tech. ● Make fists

立ち方●右四股立ち斜角
技●両手払い受け
Stance ● Right Shiko Dachi 45°
Tech. ● Double arm Harai Uke

第19挙動

第20挙動

第21挙動

裏側

立ち方●右四股立ち斜角
技●右開手中段受け、左手引き手（手
掌が上）
Stance ● Right Shiko Dachi 45°
Tech. ● Right Chudan Uke open
hand, Left Hikite

立ち方●右四股立ち斜角
技●右掛け受け
Stance ● Right Shiko Dachi 45°
Tech. ● Right Kakeuke

立ち方●右四股立ち斜角
技●右掛取り、左貫手
注意点●掛取りは脇まで引き、手掌
が下。左貫手は斜め前膝方向、肘は
身体に密着
Stance ● Right Shiko Dachi 45°
Tech. ● Right Kake Tori, left
Nukite
Point ● Pull right hand back
towards underarm, Nukite in the
same direction as front knee.
Keep left elbow against the body

第 22 挙動　　　　　第 23 挙動

中間動作

裏側

技●両手掬い受け、右足は後方を踵
蹴り
注意点●右掌上、肘締め
Tech. ● Sukuiuke right hand on
top. Kakato Keri to rear
Point ● Place right hand on top
of left hand. Don't open elbows

注意点●右掌を拳にする
Point ● Make right fist

立ち方●右摺り足立ち
技●左手添え押し突き
注意点●右拳甲を摺り合わせ、鉄槌
から正拳突き、摺り足前進
Stance ● Right Suriashi dachi
Tech. ● Right Oshi Tsuki w/ left
hand touching
Point ● Left palm stays in
contact w/ back of right hand.
Attack changes from Tettsui
into Tsuki. Step forward w/ Suriashi

第 24 挙動	第 25 挙動	第 26 挙動

裏側

立ち方●左半前屈立ち
技●後方右肘当て
注意点●左手は前方押さえ
Stance ● Left Hanzenkutsu dachi
Tech. ● Right Hijiate to the rear
Point ● Left hand keeps opponent away

立ち方●左半前屈立ち
技●右肘当て
注意点●左掌は右肘に添える。第23挙動から連続
Stance ● Left Hanzenkutsu dachi
Tech. ● Right Hijiate
Point ● Keep left palm against right elbow. Do23-25 as one combi-nation

立ち方●右斜角レの字立ち
技●右中段添え受け
注意点●左掌を右小手に沿わせて添え受け
Stance ● Right Renojidachi 45°
Tech. ● Right Chudan Soeuke
Point ● Keep left palm against right forearm

二本目 No.2

第27挙動　　　　第28挙動　　　　第29挙動

中間動作

裏側

立ち方●左四股立ち直角
技●左下段鉄槌当て
Stance ● Left Shiko Dachi 45°
Tech. ● Left Gedan Tettsui Ate

立ち方●右四股立ち直角
技●右下段払い
注意点● 27挙動と28挙動は連続。
四股立ち移動は素早く、体の上下に
注意
Stance ● Right Shiko Dachi 90°
Tech. ● Right Gedan Barai
Point ● Do 27-28 as one combination and quickly. Pay attention
to the height of your body

立ち方●左斜角レの字立ち
技●左中段添え受け
注意点●右掌を左拳に沿わせて添え
受け
Stance ● Left Renojidachi 45°
Tech. ● Left Chudan Soeuke
Point ● Keep right palm against
left forearm

第30挙動　　　第31挙動　　　第32挙動

裏側

立ち方●右四股立ち直角
技●右下段鉄槌当て
Stance ● Right Shiko Dachi 90°
Tech. ● Right Gedan Tettsui
Ate

立ち方●左四股立ち直角
技●左下段払い
注意点● 30挙動と31挙動は連続。
四股立ち移動は素早く、体の上下に
注意
Stance ● Left Shiko Dachi 90°
Tech. ● Left Gedan Barai
Point ● Do 30-31 as one combi-
naiton and quickly. Pay attention
to the height of your body

立ち方●右四股立ち直角
技●弓張りの構え
注意点●左掌で腕取り、右底掌で下
段当て。動作はゆっくり
Stance ● Right Shiko Dachi 90°
Tech. ● Yumibari no kamae
Point ● Ude tori w/ left hand
and Gedan Ate w/ right Teisho
Ate(slowly).

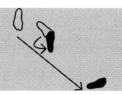 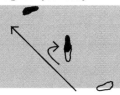 

第 33 挙動	第 34 挙動	第 35 挙動

裏側

立ち方●左四股立ち直角
技●弓張りの構え
注意点●右掌で腕取り、左底掌で下段当て。動作はゆっくり
Stance ● Left Shiko Dachi 90°
Tech. ● Yumibari no kamae
Point ● Ude Tori w/ right hand and Gedan Ate w/ left Teisho Ate (slowly).

立ち方●右摺り足立ち
技●右内小手受け
注意点●右足払いて摺り足前進。左掌に右小手を合わせる
Stance ● Right Suriashi dachi
Tech. ● Right Uchi Kote Uke
Point ● Right Ashibarai and step forward w/ Suriashi. Hit left hand w/ right forearm

立ち方●右摺り足立ち
技●右上段裏打ち
注意点●第 34 挙動と 35 挙動は連続動作
Stance ● Right Suriashi dachi
Tech. ● Right Jodan Urauchi
Point ● Do 34-35 as one combination

【分解】
Bunkai

二本目 （続き）

立ち方●右摺り足立ち
技●右上段裏打ち（引き）
Stance ● Right Suriashi dachi
Tech. ● Right Jodan Urauchi (Hiki)

立ち方●前足交差
Stance ● Cross legs (Put front foot over)

立ち方●左三戦立ち
技●左横受け右下段払い
注意点●北東の方向。ゆっくり
Stance ● Left Sanchin Dachi
Tech. ● Left Yokouke Right Gedan Barai
Point ● Turn toward northwest, slowly

第 37 挙動	第 38 挙動	第 39 挙動

中間動作

裏側

立ち方●右四股立ち直角
技●右上げ突き、左手掌は水月
注意点●左手底掌受けと同時に顎へ上げ
突き。気合
Stance ● Right Shiko Dachi 90°
Tech. ● Right Age Tsuki, put left
hand on solar plexus at the same
time
Point ● Kiai

立ち方●右四股立ち直角
技●右上段裏打ち
Stance ● Right Shiko Dachi 90°
Tech. ● Right Jodan Urauchi

立ち方●右四股立ち直角
技●右下段鉄槌打ち
Stance ● Right Shiko Dachi 90°
Tech. ● Right Gedan Tettsui
Uchi

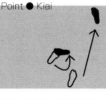

【分解】
Bunkai

三本目 No.3

第40挙動　第41挙動　第42挙動

立ち方●左四股立ち直角
技●真っすぐ後退、左下段払い
注意点●第37挙動から40挙動までは一連の動作
Stance ● Left Shiko Dachi 90°
Tech. ● Step back in a straight line. Left Gedan Barai
Point ● Do 37-40 as one combination

立ち方●右猫足立ち
技●右肘外し、後方左肘当て
注意点●猫足立ちに落とすと同時に臀部を後方へ突き出す
Stance ● Right Nekoashi dachi
Tech. ● Break grab w/ right elbow. Left Hijiate to the rear
Point ● Thrust hips to the rear while making Nekoashi dachi

立ち方●左猫足立ち
技●左肘外し、後方右肘当て
注意点●前足を後方へ下げ、猫足立ちに落とすと同時に臀部を後方へ突き出す
Stance ● Left Nekoashi dachi
Tech. ● Break grab w/ left elbow. Right Hijiate to the rear
Point ● Step back w/ right foot. Thrust hips to the rear while making Nekoashi dachi

裏側

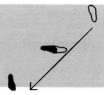

第43挙動　　　　第44挙動

中間動作

裏側

立ち方●前足交差
Stance ● Cross legs

立ち方●右三戦立ち
技●右横受け左下段払い
注意点●北西の方向、ゆっくり
Stance ● Right Sanchin Dachi
Tech. ● Right Yoko Uke and left Gedan Barai
Point●Toward northwest, slowly

立ち方●左四股立ち直角
技●左上げ突き、右手掌水月
注意点●右手底掌受けと同時に顎への上げ突き。気合
Stance ● Left Shiko Dachi 45°
Tech. ● Left Agezuki, right hand is on solar plexus at the same time
Point ● Kiai

【分解】
Bunkai

四本目 No.4

第45挙動　　　第46挙動　　　第47挙動

裏側

立ち方●左四股立ち直角
技●左上段裏打ち
Stance ● Left Shiko Dachi 90°
Tech. ● Left Jodan Urauchi

立ち方●左四股立ち直角
技●左下段鉄槌打ち
Stance ● Left Shiko Dachi 90°
Tech. ● Left Gedan Tettsui Uchi

立ち方●右四股立ち直角
技●真っすぐ後退、右下段払い
注意点●第44挙動から第47挙動まで
は一連の動作
Stance ● Right Shiko Dachi 90°
Tech. ● Step back straightly, right
Gedan Ba rai
Point ● Do 44-47 as one combination

中間動作

裏側

立ち方●左猫足立ち
技●左肘外し、後方右肘当て
注意点●猫足立ちに落とすと同時に
臀部を後方へ突き出す
Stance ● Left Nekoashi dachi
Tech. ● Break grab w/ left
elbow, Right Hijiate to the rear
Point ● Thrust hips to the rear
while making Nekoashi dachi

立ち方●右猫足立ち
技●右肘外し、後方左肘当て
注意点●猫足立ちに落とすと同時に
臀部を後方へ突き出す
Stance ● Right Nekoashi dachi
Tech. ● Break grab w/ right
elbow, Left Hijiate to the rear
Point ● Thrust hips to the rear
while making Nekoashi dachi

立ち方●右摺り足立ち
技●左底掌受け落とし、上段裏打ち
Stance ● Right Suriashi dachi
Tech. ● Left Teisho Uke Otoshi,
Right Jodan Urauchi

【分解】
Bunkai

四本目（続き）

第51挙動　　　第52挙動　　　直って

裏側

立ち方●左猫足立ち
技●両手肘、手掌合わせ
注意点●上から落とすように
Stance ● Left Nekoashi dachi
Tech. ● Bring backs of hands
and elbows together

立ち方●左猫足立ち
技●両手繰り受け
注意点●肘を左右八字に開く
Stance ● Left Nekoashi dachi
Tech. ● Double arm Kuriuke
Point ● Let elbows open away
from the body

立ち方●前足を引いて結び立ち
技●右手掌上に重ねる
息吹●呑
Stance ● Step back w/ front
foot into Musubidachi
Tech. ● Place right hand on top
of left
Ibuki ● Inhale

直って 　気を付け 　礼

中間動作

裏側

立ち方●結び立ち
技●手掌を摺り合わせて丹田集中
息吹●吐
Stance ● Musubidachi
Tech. ● Bring hands down in front of Tanden
Ibuki ● Exhale

立ち方●結び立ち
注意点●顎を引き、両手は真っすぐ伸ばして大腿側部に付ける
Stance ● Musubidachi
Point ● Pull chin back. Keep fingers straight and hands on outer thight.

立ち方●結び立ち
注意点●前方30度位、礼は深すぎない
Stance ● Musubidachi
Point ● Bow forward for 30°.Be careful not to bow too deeply

気を付け

裏側

立ち方●結び立ち
注意点●顎を引き、両手は真っすぐ
伸ばして大腿側部につける
Stance ● Musubidachi
Point ● Pull chin back. Keep
fingers straight and hands on
outer thight.

サンセール

三十六手
Sanseiru

型のポイント

　サンセールは三戦の動作から始まる四つの型（サンセール、セイサン、シソーチン、スーパーリンペイ）の内、一番初めの型で、三戦立ちでの三歩移動は三戦と全く同じ動作である。

　開手型としての三戦の動作では独自の呼吸法と極端な締めは行わず、自然呼吸による丹田集中をもって演武する。

　三戦立ち、前屈立ち、四股立ち、摺り足立ちによる東西南北を演武線とし、前蹴り、関節蹴り等の蹴り技が多く、セインチンの虎に対して、龍の型に例えられる。

　分解動作は、全日本空手道剛柔会が制定しているサンセール型分解組手（１本〜５本）から、二本目、三本目、四本目、五本目までの一部を掲載している。

Sanseiru is the first of 4 kata which start from Sanchin position. The first part of this kata is the same as the first part of Sanchin kata.

However, unlike Sanchin which uses strong Ibuki and tension, all Kaishu kata, including Sanseiru, use natural breathing with focus on Tanden.

In Sanseiru there are steps in four directions　(north, south, east, and west) performed in Sanchin Dachi, Zenkutsu Dachi, Shiko Dachi, or Suriashi Dachi. There are also many kicking techniques such as Maegeri and Kansetsu Keri.

Sanseiru is also called "Ryu no kata" (Dragon's kata), the opposite of Seinchin ("Tora no kata" or "Tiger's kata").

The Sanseiru Kata Bunkai created by the J.K.G.A. contains 5 parts all together. Pictures taken from 2, 3, 4, and 5 are included in the following pages.

気を付け　礼　気を付け

立ち方●結び立ち
注意点●顎を引き、両手は真っすぐ
伸ばして大腿側部につける
Stance ● Musubidachi
Point ● Pull chin back. Keep
fingers straight and hands on
outer thight.

立ち方●結び立ち
注意点●前方30度位、礼は深すぎ
ない
Stance ● Musubidachi
Point ● Bow forward for 30° .Be
careful not to bow too deeply

立ち方●結び立ち
Stance ● Musubidachi

裏側

<table>
<tr><td align="center">用意1</td><td align="center">用意2</td><td align="center">用意3</td></tr>
</table>

中間動作

裏側

立ち方●結び立ち
注意点●右掌内側、丹田の前で重ね
丹田集中
息吹●ゆっくり呑
Stance ● Musubidachi
Point ● Right hand on the
inside. Hands are crossed in
front of Tanden
Ibuki ● Inhale slowly

立ち方●平行立ち
注意点●爪先を支点に踵を外に開く
Stance ● Heiko Dachi
Point ● Keep balls of feet in
place and only move heels

立ち方●平行立ち
注意点●両拳は脇を締めながら体側
へ、正拳は真下へ向けて、両肩を落
とす
息吹●ゆっくり吐
Stance ● Heiko Dachi
Point ● Keep elbows against
side of body, fists pointing
straight down, and shoulders
relaxed
Ibuki ● Exhale slowly

第1挙動 第2挙動 第3挙動

立ち方●右三戦立ち
技●三戦の構え、右拳外側より両手
交差
注意点●右足を内側中心線より一歩
前進。三戦の型と同じ。
Stance ● Right Sanchin Dachi
Tech. ● Sanchin no Kamae.
Right fist goes out side
Point ● Step right foot forward
using an inward curve. Same as
Sanchin Kata.

立ち方●右三戦立ち
技●左拳　引き手
注意点●三戦の型と同じ。
Stance ● Right Sanchin Dachi
Tech. ● Left Hikite
Point ● Same as Sanchin.

立ち方●右三戦立ち
技●左拳　正拳突き
注意点●三戦の型と同じ。
Stance ● Right Sanchin Dachi
Tech. ● Left Seiken Tsuki
Point ● Same as Sanchin.

裏側

第４挙動	第５挙動	第６挙動

中間動作

裏側

立ち方●右三戦立ち
技●左拳　中段受け
注意点●三戦の型と同じ。
Stance ● Right Sanchin Dachi
Tech. ● Left Chudan Uke
Point ● Same as Sanchin.

立ち方●左三戦立ち
技●足だけ前進
注意点●三戦の型と同じ。
Stance ● Left Sanchin Dachi
Tech. ● Step left foot forward
Point ● Same as Sanchin.

立ち方●左三戦立ち
技●右拳　引き手
注意点●三戦の型と同じ。
Stance ● Left Sanchin Dachi
Tech. ● Right Hikite
Point ● Same as Sanchin.

第7挙動 第8挙動 第9挙動

立ち方●左三戦立ち
技●右拳　正拳突き
注意点●三戦の型と同じ。
Stance ● Left Sanchin Dachi
Tech. ● Right Seiken Tsuki
Point ● Same as Sanchin.

立ち方●左三戦立ち
技●右拳　中段受け
注意点●三戦の型と同じ。
Stance ● Left Sanchin Dachi
Tech. ● Right Chudan Uke
Point ● Same as Sanchin.

立ち方●右三戦立ち
技●足だけ前進
注意点●三戦の型と同じ。
Stance ● Right Sanchin Dachi
Tech. ● Step right foot forward
Point ● Same as Sanchin.

第10挙動	第11挙動	第12挙動

中間動作

裏側

立ち方●右三戦立ち
技●左拳　引き手
注意点●三戦の型と同じ。
Stance ● Right Sanchin Dachi
Tech. ● Left Hikite
Point ● Same as Sanchin.

立ち方●右三戦立ち
技●左拳　正拳突き
注意点●三戦の型と同じ。
Stance ● Right Sanchin Dachi
Tech. ● Left Seiken Tsuki
Point ● Same as Sanchin.

立ち方●右三戦立ち
技●右手　左腕上部（掌内側）
Stance ● Right Sanchin Dachi
Tech. ● Place right hand on top
of left arm (Palm facing inward)

【分解】
Bunkai

二本目 No.2

第13挙動　　　　第14挙動　　　　第15挙動

立ち方●右前屈立ち
技●右掌脚・踵掬い。左肘上部まで掬い取る。左底掌押さえ
注意点●体を正面に戻し、後足を前進。前屈立ちは深め。目線はやや前方。右掌は左底掌の内側よりかい込む
Stance ● Right Zenkutsu Dachi
Tech. ● Sukui w/ right hand to opponent's leg and heel. Then pull right hand back under left elbow
Point ● Turn body toward the front. Step into a deep Zenkutsu Dachi w/ right foot. Right hand goes inside of left Teisho

裏側

立ち方●右三戦立ち
技●右掌にて左腕上部より擦り落とし
注意点●持たれた手を外すように
Stance ● Right Sanchin Dachi
Tech. ● Suri otoshi w/ left hand
Point ● Right hand breaks grab on left arm

立ち方●左後屈立ち
技●左掌　右腕上部より擦り落とし
注意点●前足を後方に引き、腰の切り返しと同時に
Stance ● Left Zenkutsu Dachi
Tech. ● Left hand Suri otoshi from top of right arm
Point ● Step back w/ right foot while twisting hip

第 16 挙動　　　第 17 挙動

中間動作

裏側

立ち方●右前屈立ち
技●両手上段交差受け
注意点●体を真っすぐに直し、目線
は正面。両掌を上段に捻転。肘は締
める
Stance ● Right Zenkutsu Dachi
Tech. ● Double arm Jodan Kosa
Uke
Point ● Lift body straight and
look to the front. Twist wrists
while lifting hands. Keep elbows
close to the body

技●左前蹴り
Tech. ● Left Maegeri

立ち方●左三戦立ち
注意点●交差受けはそのまま
Stance ● Left Sanchin Dachi
Point ● Keep Kosa Uke

【分解】
Bunkai

三本目 No.3

第18挙動　　　　　第19挙動　　　　　第20挙動

裏側

立ち方●右前屈立ち
技●右中段肘当て
注意点●肘当ては脇を締める
Stance ● Right Zenkutsu Dachi
Tech. ● Right Chudan Hijiate
Point ● Keep elbows close to
the body

立ち方●右前屈立ち
技●左中段正拳突き
注意点●正拳突きは肘を締め正中線
Stance ● Right Zenkutsu Dachi
Tech. ● Left Chudan Tsuki
Point ● Punch center

立ち方●前足を引き上げ
注意点●右肘当て、左正拳突きのまま
Stance ● Raise front leg
Point ● Keep right Hijiate and
left Tsuki

第 21 挙動　　　　　　　　　第 22 挙動

中間動作

裏側

技●右関節蹴り
注意点●右肘当て、左正拳突きのまま
Stance ● Right Kansetsu Keri
Point ● Keep right Hijiate and
left Tsuki

立ち方●引き足
注意点●右肘当て、左正拳突きのまま
Stance ● Hikiashi
Point ● Keep right Hijiate and
left Tsuki

立ち方●左三戦立ち
技●左中段受け
注意点●蹴り足を前方で交差させて後ろに
回る。受けはゆっくり
Stance ● Left Sanchin Dachi
Tech. ● Left Chudan Uke
Point ● Cross the kicking leg in front
of the supporting leg and turn 180°

第 23 挙動　　　　第 24 挙動　　　　第 25 挙動

技●右前蹴り
注意点●蹴る時に受け手を崩さない
Tech. ● Right Maegeri
Point ● Keep block when kicking

立ち方●右前屈立ち
技●右中段肘当て
注意点●肘当ては脇を締める
Stance ● Right Zenkutsu Dachi
Tech. ● Right Chudan Hijiate
Point ● Keep elbows close to
the body

立ち方●右前屈立ち
技●左中段正拳突き
注意点●正拳突きは肘を締め正中線
Stance ● Right Zenkutsu Dachi
Tech. ● Left Chudan Tsuki
Point ● Punch center

裏側

第 26 挙動　　第 27 挙動

中間動作

裏側

立ち方●前足引き上げ
注意点●右肘当て、左正拳突きのまま
Stance ● Raise front leg
Point ● Keep right Hijiate and
left Tsuki

技●右関節蹴り
注意点●右肘当て、左正拳突きのまま
Tech. ● Raise Kansetsu Keri
Point ● Keep right Hijiate and
left Tsuki

立ち方●引き足
注意点●右肘当て、左正拳突きのまま
Stance ● Hikiashi
Point ● Keep right Hijiate and
left Tsuki

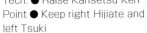

第 28 挙動　　　第 29 挙動　　　第 30 挙動

立ち方●左三戦立ち
技●左中段受け
注意点●蹴り足を右前方に置き西に転身。
受けはゆっくり
Stance ● Left Sanchin Dachi
Tech. ● Left Chudan Uke
Point ● Put kicking leg down in
front and to the right, and turn west

技●右前蹴り
注意点●蹴る時に受けを崩さない
Tech. ● Right Maegeri
Point ● Keep block when kicking

立ち方●右前屈立ち
技●右中段肘当て
注意点●肘当ては肘を締める
Stance ● Raise Zenkutsu Dachi
Tech. ● Right Chudan Hijiate
Point ● Be careful of keeping
elbow close

裏側

第31挙動	第32挙動	第33挙動

中間動作

裏側

立ち方●右前屈立ち
技●左中段正拳突き
注意点●正拳突きは肘を締め正中線
Stance ● Right Zenkutsu Dachi
Tech. ● Left Chudan Tsuki
Point ● Punch center

立ち方●前足を引き上げ
注意点●右肘当て、正拳突きのまま
Stance ● Raise front leg
Point ● Keep right Hijiate and
left Tsuki

技●右関節蹴り
注意点●右肘当て、正拳突きのまま
Tech. ● Right Kansetsu Keri
Point ● Keep right Hijiate and
left Tsuki

第34挙動　　　第35挙動

裏側

立ち方●引き足
注意点●右肘当て、正拳突きのまま
Stance ● Hikiashi
Point ● Keep right Hijiate and left Tsuki

立ち方●左三戦立ち
技●左中段受け
注意点●蹴り足を左前方に交差、真後ろ東に転身。受けはゆっくり
Stance ● Left Sanchin Dachi
Tech. ● Left Chudan Uke
Point ● Put kicking leg in front and to the left, and turn east. Block slowly

立ち方●左三戦立ち
技●右前蹴り
注意点●蹴る時に受け手を崩さない
Stance ● Left Sanchin Dachi
Tech. ● Right Maegeri
Point ● Keep block when kicking

第36挙動	第37挙動	第38挙動

中間動作

裏側

立ち方●右前屈立ち
技●右中段肘当て
注意点●肘当ては脇を締める
Stance ● Right Zenkutsu Dachi
Tech. ● Right Chudan Hijiate
Point ● Keep elbows closed

立ち方●右前屈立ち
技●左中段正拳突き
注意点●正拳突きは肘を締め正中線
Stance ● Right Zenkutsu Dachi
Tech. ● Left Chudan Tsuki
Point ● Punch center

立ち方●四股立ち平角
技●両手開手引き手
注意点●頭部の高さを変えず体と目線を
北に向ける
Stance ● Shiko Dachi 180°
Tech. ● Double arm Hikite with
open hands
Point ● Turn body and face north.
Don't change the height of head

【分解】
Bunkai

四本目 No.4

第 39 挙動　　　　　　　　　　　第 40 挙動

立ち方●四股立ち平角
技●両手開手交差
注意点●右手外側で手掌を外に向けて両
手を交差
Stance ● Shiko Dachi 180°
Tech. ● Cross open hands
Point ● Right hand on top of left.
Palm facing up

立ち方●四股立ち平角
技●両手拳引き手
注意点●右足を直線で後方に引き、
真後ろ南に四股立ちで移動
Stance ● Shikodchi 180°
Tech. ● Double arm Hikite
Point ● Right foot crosses
straight behind left foot into
Shiko Dachi facing south

立ち方●四股立ち平角
技●両手拳交差落とし
注意点●両手拳を内外入れ換えて交差
落とし。右手内側。両拳とも拳甲が正面
Stance ● Shiko Dachi 180°
Tech. ● Double arm Kosa otoshi
Point ● Left hand on top of right.
The backs of hands facing front

  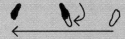

第41挙動　　　　　第42挙動

中間動作

裏側

立ち方●四股立ち平角
技●両手掌を上下に合わせる（右が上）
注意点●四股立ちを北に戻し、内から外（肘
から手掌）へ両手掴み取り。目線は東から北
Stance ● Shiko Dachi 180°
Tech. ● Place right hand above left
Point ● Look east, and then north.
Hands move from elbows to center of
body into Tsukami tori

立ち方●右足払い
技●両手拳引き手
注意点●足払いと同時に両拳を引き、体
と目線を東に向ける
Stance ● Right Ashibarai
Tech. ● Doubule arm Hikite
Point ● Do Ashibarai and double
Hikite at the same time while
turning eyes and body east

第 43 挙動　　第 44 挙動　　第 45 挙動

 裏側

立ち方●右摺り足立ち
技●両手突き
注意点●両手突きの拳は正中線（左拳上）。
気合
Stance ● Right Suriashi dachi
Tech. ● Morote Tsuki
Point ● Both fists on center line of
the body (left fist on to). Kiai

立ち方●左三戦立ち
技●左中段受け
注意点●右足を前方で交差、西に回転。
受けはゆっくり
Stance ● Right Sanchin Dachi
Tech. ● Left Chudan Uke
Point ● Cross right foot in front of
left and turn toward west. Block
slowly.

立ち方●右三戦立ち
技●右中段受け
注意点●右足を前進。受けはゆっくり
Stance ● Right Sanchin Dachi
Tech. ● Right Chudan Uke
Point ● Step w/ right foot forward.
Block slowly

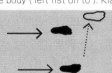

第 46 挙動　　　第 47 挙動

中間動作

裏側

立ち方●四股立ち平角
技●両手掌を上下に合わせる（左が上）
注意点●四股立ちにしながら両手掴み取り（肘から手掌）。目線は西から北
Stance ● Shiko Dachi 180°
Tech. ● Place left hand above right
Point ● Making Shiko Dachi, hands go to Tsukami tori. Look west and then north.

立ち方●左足払い
技●両手拳引き手
注意点●足払いと同時に両拳を引き、体と目線を西に向ける
Stance ● Left Ashibarai
Tech. ● Double arm Hikite
Point ● Do Ashibarai and double Hikite at the same time while turning eyes and body west

【分解】
Bunkai

五本目 No.5

第48挙動　　　　第49挙動　　　　直って

立ち方●左摺り足立ち
技●両手突き
注意点●両手突きの拳は正中線（右拳上）。気合
Stance ● Left Suriashi dachi
Tech. ● Morote Tsuki
Point ● Both fists on center line of the body (right fist on to). Kiai

立ち方●四股立ち斜角
技●両手鶴頭受け、犬の構え
注意点●両手を交差して右手内側より両手鶴頭による弧受け、左手は水月
Stance ● Shiko Dachi 45°
Tech. ● Ryote Kakuto Uke, Inu no Kamae
Point ● Cross hands w/ right hand inside. Make Kakuto w/ both hands. And do Kouke. Place left hand on solar plexus

立ち方●前足を引いて結び立ち
技●右手掌上に重ねる
息吹●呑
Stance ● Step back w/ right foot into Musubidachi
Tech. ● Place right hand on top of left
Ibuki ● Inhale

裏側

直って   気を付け   礼

中間動作

裏側

立ち方●結び立ち
技●手掌を摺り合わせて丹田集中
息吹●吐
Stance ● Musubidachi
Tech. ● Bring hands down in front of Tanden
Ibuki ● Exhale

立ち方●結び立ち
注意点●顎を引き、両手は真っすぐ伸ばして大腿側部に付ける
Stance ● Musubidachi
Point ● Pull chin back. Keep fingers straight and hands on outer thight.

立ち方●結び立ち
注意点●前方30度位、礼は深すぎない
Stance ● Musubidachi
Point ● Bow forward for 30° .Be careful not to bow too deeply

【分解】
Bunkai

気を付け

裏側

立ち方●結び立ち
注意点●顎を引き、両手は真っすぐ
伸ばして大腿側部につける
Stance ● Musubidachi
Point ● Pull chin back. Keep
fingers straight and hands on
outer thight.

監修・演武　Supervisor, Demonstrator

山口 剛史 （本名　紘史）
Goshi Hirofumi Yamaguchi

1942 年 9 月 28 日、満洲　新京にて誕生

全日本空手道剛柔会会祖・山口剛玄の三男として、父を補佐し、国内外の指導に
あたる。

1990 年、「全日本空手道剛柔会」、「国際空手道剛柔会」宗家として会長・最高
師範に就任。

（財）全日本空手道連盟公認　全国指導員、全国審判員、資格審査委員

世界空手道連合　元国際審判員

（財）日本体育協会　上級コーチ、A 級スポーツ指導員

Born on September 28, 1942 in Manchukuo.

He is the third son of Gogen Yamaguchi, the founder and grand master of the
Japan Karatedo Gojukai Association. He has taught both domestically and
overseas helping his father.

In 1990, he became the president and head instructor of the Japan Karatedo
Gojukai Association (J.K.G.A.) and the International Karatedo Gojukai
Association (I.K.G.A.)

Japan Karatedo Federation Instructor, Referee, and Examiner

W.U.K.O. Internatinal referee (retired)

JASA coach, JASA instructor

演武 Demonstrator

斉藤 彰宏
Akihiro Saito

1969 年 2 月 23 日生
6 歳より空手道を修業、高校生・大学生時代は
各種選手権大会、国体等で優勝、入賞。
全日本空手道連盟ナショナルチーム在籍中、各
種国際大会、国際交流遠征に参加。
全日本空手道剛柔会理事、強化委員
師範錬士五段。
Born on February 23, 1969. Started karate at
age 6. During his years as a high school and
university student, he won 1st place at many
championships including national events.
Was a member of the J.K.F. national team and
participated in international competitions
Director of J.K.G.A., member of coaching
comitee
5 dan, Shihan Renshi

演武 Demonstrator

山口 剛平 （本名　たかひら）
Gohei Takahira Yamaguchi

1976 年 2 月 14 日生
幼少 4 歳より祖父山口剛玄、父山口剛史の指
導を受け、国際空手道剛柔会世界大会・分解組
手優勝、型第 3 位。全日本空手道剛柔会全国大
会型 4 回連続優勝。
国際空手道剛柔会・全日本空手道剛柔会指導者
として国内外指導。
全日本空手道剛柔会事務局次長、四段助教。
Born on February 14, 1976. Studied karate
under his grandfather Gogen Yamaguchi and
his father Goshi Yamaguchi from the age of 4.
Won 1st place in Bunkai Kumite, and 3rd place
in Kata at the I.K.G.A. World Championships.
Won 1st place 4 years in a row at the J.K.G.A.
All Japan Championships, in individual kata.
Vice bureau chief of J.K.G.A.
4 dan, Jokyo

Made in United States
Troutdale, OR
12/09/2023

15596288R00131